Fairs Fair   T $60.00

1582480125
Hickcox, David H.
Great Northern Steam & Electric in color

D1790917

GREAT NORTHERN
Steam & Electric In Color

David H. Hickcox

The Great Northern was instrumental in the establishment of Glacier National Park. Not only did the GN actively promote tourism, it built hotels and chalets in the park, advertised Glacier Park extensively and adopted the mountain goat as its corporate symbol. In a view from a 1924 GN booklet titled *The Call of the Mountains: Vacations in Glacier National Park*, Rocky surveys his domain.

Copyright © 1999
Morning Sun Books, Inc.

All rights reserved. This book may not be reproduced in part or in whole without written permission from the publisher, except in the case of brief quotations or reproductions of the cover for the purposes of review.

Published by
Morning Sun Books, Inc.
9 Pheasant Lane
Scotch Plains, NJ 07076

Library of Congress
Catalog Card No. 98-066804

First Printing
ISBN 1-58248-012-5

Color separation and printing by
The Kutztown Publishing Co., Inc.
Kutztown, Pennsylvania

DEDICATION
To Barbara who means so much.

ACKNOWLEDGEMENTS

Working with color photography of the Great Northern Railway has indeed been a privilege. I am especially indebted to the photographers who took the time and effort to record the steam and electric operations of the Great Northern as well as those who loaned their collections: Ed Austin, Don Ball, Steve Bogen, J.J. Buckley, Gayle Christen, Marvin H. Cohen, Robert F. Collins, Martin Evoy III, Luther George, Sanford Goodrick, Carl Hehl, W.C. Janssen, Lloyd Keyser, Robert Morrison, William J. McChesney, Art Peterson, Jack Pfeifer, Russ Porter, Monty Powell, J. Schmitt, Lou Schmitz, James P. Shuman, Henry Stange, the Union Pacific Railroad Museum, Eugene Van Dusen, Bob Wanner, Bob Wason, and W. Woelfer. Bob Yanosey ("On-time Bob"), publisher of Morning Sun books, collected most of the photographs, was the driving force behind this book and brought everything together in magnificent color. Barbara Williams and Dorothy Carina of Ohio Wesleyan University, no strangers to these books, did all the word processing and made the author far more efficient than he really is.

Anyone reading this book who is not a member of the Great Northern Railway Historical Society should be. The GNRHS has published a wealth of information on the Great Northern that is not readily available elsewhere. I have used several of their Reference Sheets in preparing this volume. Their annual meetings provide an opportunity to spend a few days with fellow Great Northern fans. For membership information contact the GNRHS Secretary at 1781 Griffith, Berkley, MI 48072. The GNRHS is an excellent organization and deserves your support.

My fascination (some would say obsession) with the Great Northern began in 1971 when, just back from a year in Viet Nam with the 101st Airborne Division and immediately after getting married, I moved to Montana to begin graduate studies at the University of Montana. While our stay in Montana lasted only a few years, it has affected us ever since on both a professional and personal level. I would like to repay debts accumulated during our residency in Montana and on numerous subsequent visits by thanking a few people whose efforts went above and beyond the call of duty. John Crowley and Chris Field, faculty members in the Geography Department at the University of Montana, had an influence far greater than they suspect. I appreciate all they did to mold me into a professional geographer and I especially appreciate the friendly and mentoring manner in which they did it. These two teachers, scholars, and friends, now retired, are what education is all about. Dr. Bob and Ann Spierling of Missoula took us under their wing and always had the welcome sign out, for both short and long stays, whether or not we were expected. They treated us like family—and still do! We forgive them for purchasing a Northern Pacific, instead of a Great Northern, caboose for their bunkhouse at Flathead Lake. Gerry and Barb Murphy of Billings probably think that we regard them as innkeepers, given the number of times we have begged a bed and a hot shower after a few weeks in the field. Many thanks to Bob, Ann, Gerry and Barb for all they have done. They personify Montana hospitality at its best and we cherish their friendship through the years.

I would also like to acknowledge the contributions of two model railroaders. Gary Salzgaber of Urbana, Ohio, builder of a marvelous HO Pennsy empire, makes life bearable during the winter by letting me run the orange and green past his position light signals. There is still a mountain goat hiding in the forests on his layout. Jim Ferguson, who lives in suburbs of Troy, Vermont, and the builder of an equally impressive HO Great Northern empire, allows me to operate his beautiful layout during the summer months. Jim, a hard-core operator, conspires all winter to design new schedules and switching procedures guaranteed to confuse me. Since most of my book writing occurs during the summer, it is quite an experience to write about the Great Northern, then spend several hours operating what I just wrote about. I deeply appreciate the friendship and courtesies extended by these gentlemen.

As noted above, this book is dedicated to my wife Barbara. Without her love, support, patience, and tolerance, this book, as well as the other Morning Sun books I have done, would never have been completed. The Highway of Life is often bumpy and marred by potholes and occasional detours. Barbara smooths out the bumps, fills the potholes and makes sure we get back on the road to continue our journey. Barbara and I met on a cold and snowy night in February, 1969 in Stuttgart, Germany. I, a Second Lieutenant in the Army, was pulling OD duty for the Air Force and she, a First Lieutenant in the Army Nurse Corps (she has outranked me ever since!!) arrived on an Air Force plane from England. As part of my official duties I had to meet and greet a general in the English Army and get him on his way to Headquarters, European Command. American women were a scarcity in Stuttgart in 1969 and after getting the general on his way I introduced myself to Barbara and offered whatever services the exalted office of the Stuttgart Airfield's Officer of the Day could provide. And the rest, as they say, is history. It has been quite a journey. Whatever success I have had in my life reflects as much on Barbara as it does on me. However, she still won't let me have a mountain goat! Thus Chessie II has assumed the role of primary stress reliever.

Thanks again to the photographers whose marvelous photographs make this book what it is. Give them their deserved accolades. I take responsibility for whatever errors may have crept into this book.

GREAT NORTHERN *Steam & Electric*

STEAM OPERATIONS 6
- CLASS A · 0-6-0 8
- CLASS C · 0-8-0 9
- CLASS H · 4-6-2 15
- CLASS M · 2-6-8-0 19
- CLASS N · 2-8-8-0 20
- CLASS O · 2-8-2 23
- CLASS Q · 2-10-2 51
- CLASS R · 2-8-8-2 54
- CLASS S · 4-8-4 58
- Belpaire Boilers & Lumber 64
- The End of Steam 66

ELECTRIC OPERATIONS 72
- Disposal of the Electrics 124
- Tower Car 126

GREAT NORTHERN
Steam & Electric
In Color

The Great Northern Railway developed from the St. Paul, Minneapolis, and Manitoba Railway. The Manitoba had been organized by James J. Hill and others in 1879 from a bankrupt Minnesota railroad, the St. Paul and Pacific. It developed slowly over a ten year period, building branch lines into fertile grain producing regions such as the Red River Valley. Financed conservatively, the railroad spread slowly across North Dakota.

For some years Hill had visions of extending the Manitoba west to the Rocky Mountains and the Pacific Ocean. The Saint Paul, Minneapolis, and Manitoba became the basis for the expansion, supplying the cash reserves and credit resources necessary for such a large undertaking. Hill's strategy was to build a line west between the territory served by the Northern Pacific to the south and the Canadian Pacific to the north, and in the process eliminate the Soo Line from expanding west on a parallel route.

Thus what we now know as the Great Northern began to take shape. As the Great Northern built westward, its tracks passed through a region that was either wilderness, or at best, sparsely populated. Eastern Montana, a vast expanse of semiarid grassland, was still home to several tribes of Indians and the Rocky Mountains were a primeval wilderness with only isolated, small settlements scattered about valley floors. The Inland Empire had yet to become an empire, and the Cascade Range presented a formidable barrier to any railroad desirous of reaching the Pacific Coast. Hill's railroad was, people said, a railroad that would lead from nowhere, through nothing to nowhere. But where most people saw wilderness, Jim Hill saw commercial forests and mines. Where people saw a desert, Jim Hill saw farms. Hill was a master at judging a territory not for what it was, but for what it could become. Furthermore, Hill surmised that a well constructed railroad with low grades and easy curves could draw upon traffic created along its line and effectively compete with other transcontinental railroads.

As Hill was building his railroad across North Dakota, he financed the Montana Central which linked Butte, Helena, and Great Falls, and would eventually tie in with the Manitoba. By this method a railroad, complete with spurs to mines, smelters, wheat fields and cattle ranges, would provide traffic for the Manitoba when it reached Montana. Hill began building west from Minot, North Dakota on April 1, 1887, having secured from the federal government a right-of-way across the extensive Indian reservations of eastern Montana. The route into Montana closely followed the one surveyed by Isaac I. Stevens in 1855. The gentle gradient of the Missouri River was followed west to the Milk River which was followed to Fort Assiniboine (near present-day Havre). From Fort Assiniboine the rails were pushed south to connect with the Montana Central at Great Falls.

In 1889 the Seattle and Montana Railway Company was organized to build from Seattle to Vancouver and east across the Cascades from Everett. In the same year the Great Northern Railway Company was organized and became the controlling power of 2,770 miles of Hill-controlled railroads. In 1890 the Great Northern began building westward from Havre, the goal being to complete the line to the Pacific coast. The GN crossed the Rocky Mountains by way of Marias pass, discovered by John F. Stevens, chief engineer of the Great Northern, on December 11, 1889. Stevens legendary find enabled the Great Northern to cross the Continental Divide at an elevation of 5,215 feet, a low crossing with grades far superior to the other transcontinental railroads. Although a direct crossing of the numerous mountain ranges west of the Continental Divide was constructed, it was soon abandoned for a water-level route winding along river valleys.

The Great Northern then plotted a route across Washington which would provide it with a competitive advantage over the Northern Pacific. Tapping Spokane, the capital of the rapidly developing Inland Empire, the route cut across the area called the Big Bend Country. This not only gave it a shorter route than the Northern Pacific, which looped much further to the south, but also bisected an area served by Northern Pacific branch lines.

The Great Northern chose a route, again located by John F. Stevens, across the Cascade Mountains which, while relatively low in elevation, was plagued with heavy snowfall and steep grades. A series of switchbacks across the Cascades were completed in 1893, providing the last link between St. Paul and Seattle.

Between 1880 and 1920 a tremendous economic expansion occurred in the territory along the Great Northern's tracks. Probably nowhere else in North America is there a better example of how a railroad influenced settlement and economic development. And since the Great Northern was largely an extension of Jim Hill, seldom has one individual left his mark so deeply imprinted upon the land.

(continued on page 4)

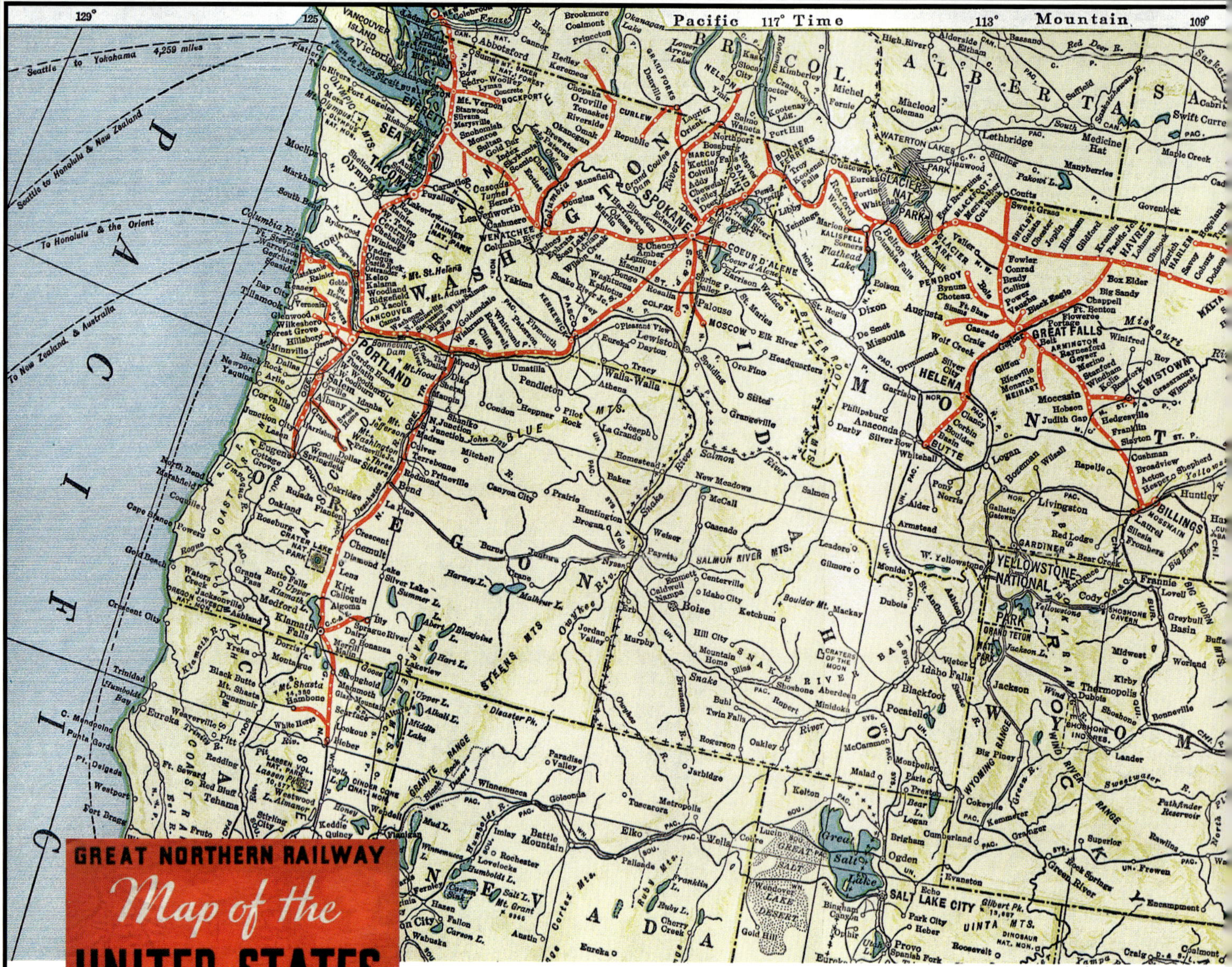

LEFT & ABOVE • The Great Northern promoted the territory it served and published a large variety of pamphlets which had maps and descriptions of the country it passed through. The more spectacular the scenery, the greater the number of pamphlets! This pamphlet contained a color map of the United States with the GN's routes highlighted and also included a capsule summary of the territory which the EMPIRE BUILDER passed through.

(continued from page 4)

Jim Hill hated empty box cars travelling across his railroad. In the early days of the Great Northern, when the traffic pattern was loads west, empties east, Hill saw a lot of empty box cars. Sometimes alone, sometimes in association with others, Hill attempted to develop the resources of the Great Northern's hinterland so that the railroad grew as the land developed. Thus the enormous iron ore deposits of the Mesabi Range became an extremely lucrative source of traffic for the Great Northern and a vast network of branch-lines were built in Minnesota and North Dakota to funnel huge amounts of wheat to market. In the space of a few short years Hill turned the vast emptiness of eastern Montana into a landscape of small farms with towns spaced every five or six miles. "Wrong side up" said the Indians when they saw the grass-lands plowed under. "Loaded box cars" was Hill's reply. The Columbia Plateau was also transformed into one of the country's premier wheat-growing regions. Alluvial valleys in Montana and Washington were turned into gardens and orchards by the diversion of rivers and the building of dams. The forests of Montana, Idaho and Washington soon felt the axe of the lumberjack. Granted a preferential freight rate so as to be competitive in the Midwest, western lumber soon travelled east by the trainload.

Settlers poured out onto the Great Plains. The government promised them land and "agricultural scientists" promised them fertile soils, abundant rainfall and bountiful yields. Honyockers, bohunk, scissorbill and nester they were derisively called by the cowboys, and Jim Hill brought them to the Northern Plains by the tens of thousands. With a bag of seed, a horse, and a plow, they set to fencing and plowing the open range in search of their own American dream. "Experts" praised the virtues and promises of dry-land farming.

Experimental farms were built, articles were written, demonstration trains toured parts of the country, and immigration agents were hired to see that prospective settlers got the word. Reduced rates were set to lure the "honyockers" west.

Towns developed along the Great Northern and these new towns served as focal points for the development of the hinterland. The towns along the Great Northern, especially in Montana, often contained almost all of the industrial, educational, health, government, social and business functions to be found in the region. The rapid development of settlement along the Great Northern is remarkable in that it developed without the impetus provided by government land grants. The Northern Pacific, Union Pacific, and Santa Fe all received land grants to finance railroad construction as well as to help settle the railroad's hinterland.

The Great Northern developed along with the territory it served. New types of steam locomotives were needed for mountainous regions. More powerful locomotives were required to pull longer and heavier trains. A more efficient crossing of the Cascades was necessary in order to alleviate the bottleneck caused by the difficult operating conditions.

Across the system curves and grades needed to be reduced.

The development of the Great Northern's steam locomotives and the construction of the Cascade Tunnel and electrification of the GN's route through the Cascade Range are two subjects of special interest to Great Northern fans.

> This book provides a review of Great Northern's steam locomotives and electric operations during the age of color photography. Covering the years from 1949 to 1957, and focusing on the 1950's, a representative view of Great Northern's steam and electric operations in the years before dieselization is provided. While color views of Great Northern steam and electric operations are rare, we have attempted to provide an "everyday" view of how the Great Northern went about its business; a view that most of us can only dream about.
>
> The Great Northern's steam and electric operations ended within a year of each other. Arguably the most fascinating and unique aspect of the Great Northern, neither steam nor electric was profusely photographed in color. The pages that follow are a tribute to the photographers who sought out both Great Northern steam and electric operations. The Great Northern was their adventure as much as Jim Hill's. I hope it is your adventure as well.

BIBLIOGRAPHY

Drury, George H. Guide to North American Steam Locomotives: History and Development of Steam Power Since 1900. Waukesha, Wisconsin: Kalmbach Publications, 1993.

Hickcox, David H. GN Color Guide To Freight and Passenger Equipment. Edison, New Jersey: Morning Sun Books, 1995.

Hickcox, David H. "The Impact of the Great Northern Railway on Settlement in Northern Montana, 1880-1920". Railroad History, 148 (Spring, 1983).

Hidy, Ralph, Muriel E. Hidy, Roy V. Scott with Don L. Hofsommer. The Great Northern Railway, A History. Boston: Harvard Business School Press, 1988.

Keyes, Norman C. Jr. and Kenneth R. Middleton. The Great Northern Railway Company: All-Time Locomotive Roster, 1861-1970. Railroad History, No. 143 (Autumn, 1980).

Keyes, Norman C., et al. "The Great Northern 2-8-8-0". Great Northern Historical Society Reference Sheet No. 29.

Kautz, Robert E. "Great Northern's Appleyard". Great Northern Historical Society Reference Sheet No. 92, September, 1994.

Keillor, Garrison. Lake Wobegon Days. New York: Penguin Books, 1986.

Malone, Michael P. James J. Hill. Norman, University of Oklahoma Press, 1996.

Martin, Charles F. Locomotives of the Empire Builder: A Railbuff's Primer of Steam on the Great Northern Railway. Chicago: Normandie House, 1972.

McGinley, William A., Michael D. Oltman, and James Vyerberg. "Great Northern Three-Phase Electric Locomotive." Great Northern Historical Society Reference Sheet No. 18.

Middleton, William D. When The Steam Railroads Electrified. Milwaukee, Wisconsin: Kalmbach Publishing Co., 1974.

Peterka, Dale. "Great Northern Steam Locomotives Classes P-1 and P-2". Great Northern Historical Society Reference Sheet No. 174, March, 1991.

Peterka, Dale. "Great Northern's Z-1 Class Electric Locomotives." Great Northern Historical Society Reference Sheet No. 210, December, 1993.

Priebe, Norman F. "Great Northern Steam Locomotive, Class O-8, 2-8-2." Great Northern Railway Historical Society Reference Sheet No. 98, June 1985.

Priebe, Norman F. "Steam's Last Days on the Great Northern." Great Northern Railway Historical Society Reference Sheet No. 124, September, 1987

Townsend, Charles. "Great Northern Modernized Class Y-1 Electrics." Great Northern Historical Society Reference Sheet No. 58.

Westinghouse Electric & Manufacturing Co. The Great Northern Railway Electrification. Special Publication No. 1857, September, 1929.

Wood, Charles and Dorothy. The Great Northern Railway, A Pictorial Study. Edmonds, Washington: Pacific Fast Mail, 1979.

Wood, Charles R. Lines West. Burbank, California: Superior Press, 1967.

GREAT NORTHERN STEAM OPERATIONS

A study of the Great Northern's policy towards the development of steam locomotives reveals one constant: the theme of increased efficiency and economy. Jim Hill's philosophy towards the operation of the Great Northern emphasized maximum ton mileage with minimum train miles. Thus steam locomotives were designed to meet the Great Northern's requirements, both in terms of the reality of the railroad's physical needs as well as its operating philosophy. The locomotives themselves would acquire characteristics which would give them their own unique appearance. The defining characteristic for most of the Great Northern's modern steam power was the Belpaire firebox, used extensively only on the GN and the Pennsylvania Railroad. Operating conditions also played a major role in steam locomotive development on the GN. West of Minot there were long straight stretches of track ascending towards the Rockies and culminating in Marias Pass. The territory between Spokane and Wenatchee, Washington also favored fast running locomotives that had power to pull. The operating conditions in Stevens Pass, Jim Hill's achilles heel, severely taxed GN's motive power and was not completely solved until the completion of the Cascade Tunnel and electrification between Wenatchee and Skykomish. Thus, once the Great Northern built west from North Dakota, it encountered operating conditions that required several different types of steam locomotives. The need to maximize ton miles with minimum train miles continued to define the Great Northern's motive power needs.

While the Belpaire firebox served as a defining characteristic on most classes of GN steam locomotives (it first appeared in 1898 on 4-8-0's built by Brooks), there were other features the GN adopted. Locomotive boosters, superheaters and brick arches in the firebox contributed towards increased power and fuel efficiency. Beginning in the 1920's, Vanderbilt tenders were utilized although many smaller locomotives had boxy, rectangular tenders. In 1921, when the price of oil fell dramatically, the Great Northern converted many steam locomotives to oil burners. By 1931 almost one third of the roster burned oil. With locomotive fuel constituting 15 percent of operating costs and with most locomotive coal coming from off line (only lower BTU lignite was available on line), oil was especially attractive. To further increase efficiency and reduce cost the capacities of tenders were increased and underutilized water and coal stations were closed. The number of operating divisions was reduced from sixteen in 1920 to eight in 1935. Further modifications to steam locomotives involved utilizing automatic fire doors, power-reverse gears, feed-water heaters, exhaust steam injectors, and power-grate shakers. These devices saved fuel, increased the locomotives' performance and generally boosted morale of the engine crews.

The placement of air pumps on the front of the smokebox further contributed to a Great Northern "look". The air pumps displaced the headlight to a location centered below the air pumps, or on the articulateds, the pilot deck, another GN characteristic. The front of modern Great Northern locomotives had a no nonsense look to them which gave an impression of strength and power. With a "brutish" type of appearance and Belpaire fireboxes, most GN steam not only had a unique appearance but were often characterized by a lack of aesthetics—non GN fans use the word "homely" when they want to be generous. While beauty is in the eyes of the beholder and function dominates form (aesthetics of steam locomotives certainly did not effect the Great Northern's bottom line!) the two classes of modern GN steam power which utilized the conventional radial stay firebox, the P-2 Mountains and S-2 Northerns, are considered by many to be the most visually appealing steam locomotives rostered by the GN.

The appearance of Great Northern steam locomotives was enhanced by the Rocky Mountain Goat herald which was applied to tenders beginning in the 1920's. Replacing "Great Northern" stenciled on the tender's flanks, the herald was distinctive and offered instant recognition. Later, red was added making it quite attractive. Steam locomotives were generally painted light olive green on the boiler and aluminum on the smokebox with individual shops often adding their own touch, such as red cab roofs. The famous "Glacier Park" paint scheme was never officially recognized by GN management.

The Great Northern favored Baldwin Locomotive Works over Lima and Alco for its steam locomotives. After 1900, the latter two companies only built a few dozen locomotives for the GN. Always with an eye towards the bottom line, the Great Northern used its shops to not only rebuild steam locomotives but also to build locomotives from the ground up.

In keeping with its corporate nature, Great Northern steam locomotives were conservative in their design. Both the GN's philosophy and its operating conditions favored keeping as much weight as possible on the driving wheels. Whether lugging iron ore to the docks at Allouez, freight across the Dakota and Montana grasslands, or tonnage over Stevens Pass, the Great Northern needed tractive effort and lots of it. Thus the GN came to rely on wheel arrangements that favored keeping the locomotive's weight on the drivers. No modern freight locomotives had four wheel lead or trailing trucks. Indeed, as the Great Northern was concerned, the fewer trailing axles the better (it was almost as if Jim Hill had said "Give me locomotives to match my mountains"). Thus 2-8-8-0's, 2-8-8-2's and 2-6-8-0's, with massive amounts of tractive effort, were built. They lugged the freight rather than speeding it to its destination, but they produced maximum ton miles with minimum train miles.

In the early 1900's trains became heavier and longer which prompted the Great Northern to develop larger and more powerful steam locomotives. In 1906 five 2-6-6-2's were acquired for helper service in Stevens Pass and these were followed in 1907 and 1908 by an additional forty five for road service. In 1906 and 1907 150 2-6-2's were purchased, although they later proved to be unsatisfactory. The GN first purchased 2-8-2's in 1911, the first of many. Between 1919 and 1931 the GN acquired or built 158 locomotives. Fifty 2-8-2's were purchased in 1919 and 1920, thirty 2-10-2's in 1923, and four 2-8-8-2's in 1924. These were followed by twenty six 2-8-8-2's between 1927 and 1930. The 2-8-8-2's replaced the 2-6-6-2's and 2-6-8-0's, both of which were rebuilt as 2-8-2's. The GN received twenty eight 4-8-2's in 1923 and twenty 4-8-4's in 1929 and 1930 for high speed passenger service.

Despite this influx of new power, in 1921 the most common steam locomotive was the 2-8-0 that had an average tractive effort of 37,500 pounds. However, by 1931 the Great Northern rostered 411 modern steam locomotives and only 150 2-8-0's. Between 1919 and 1931 the number of steam locomotives decreased from 1,391 to 1,087 but the average tractive effort increased 30 percent, reflecting the modern 2-8-0's average tractive effort of 63,000 pounds and the 2-8-8-2's average 114,000 pounds of tractive effort. In 1931, 97 percent of the Great Northern's locomotive roster was steam. Minot was the watershed of steam locomotive assignments with heavier power assigned west of Minot and lighter power used east to the Twin Cities. The major exception to this was, of course, the movement of iron ore from the Mesabi Range to the ore docks at Superior, handled mostly by the massive 2-8-8-0's.

Class O-8 Mikados, built by the GN's shops in 1931-1932 are generally considered the highlight of steam development on the Great Northern. The 0-8's were "super power GN style" in the words of GN historian

GREAT NORTHERN RAILWAY
STEAM LOCOMOTIVES

Charles R. Wood. Truly a tribute to those that designed and built them, the marvelous Mikes were the last new steam design on the GN although rebuilding and modernization programs would keep the shop forces busy for years to come.

Although the Great Northern's first diesel, a rather homely 600 horsepower boxcab, was purchased in 1926, dieselization proceeded slowly. Indeed, due to World War II and the difficulty the GN had with the War Production Board, which allocated diesels to the nation's railroads during World War II, dieselization proceeded much slower than management preferred. Colorful orange and green cab units began appearing on the GN in numbers after World War II. In 1951 the Great Northern still rostered 511 steam locomotives (and twenty electrics which would also succumb to the diesel's superior operating efficiencies) but the handwriting was on the wall. In 1954 management decided to retire all steam power as soon as feasible. Fortunately for steam fans in the upper Midwest, traffic surges kept steam operating until 1957 when the last fire was dropped. Discussed extensively in the following pictures and text, the demise of steam was an event which would change forever the character and face of the Great Northern. The end of steam was inevitable, a result of the Great Northern's never-ending quest for efficiency and the maximization of ton miles with minimum train miles. The end of steam was an emotional time for both GN fans and railfans in general. In the words of the authors of *The Great Northern Railway, A History* "....not even the most dedicated industrial engineer could feel for internal combustion the primeval excitement set off by an R-2 starting a tonnage train or an S-2 running at track speed."

Steam locomotives in this volume are arranged by the classification system adopted by the Great Northern in 1903. After each heading for steam class types the photo/description from the GN Public Relations Department pictorial brochure *Great Northern Railway Steam Locomotives* (pictured above) is included. The standard reference for GN steam locomotives, as well as electrics and diesels, is Norman C. Keyes, Jr. and Kenneth R. Middleton, *The Great Northern Railway Company: All-Time Locomotive Roster, 1861-1970*. Originally published as Volume 143 of Railroad History, the 176 page roster is available for $13.50 from the GNRHS at the address printed on page 2.

GREAT NORTHERN STEAM LOCOMOTIVES PICTURED IN THIS VOLUME

Class A-9, 0-6-0
1-94, not complete, 56 locomotives built by GN, BLW, Rogers, 1903-1912
380-399, Baldwin, 1912

Class C-1, 0-8-0
810-849, Baldwin, 1918

Class C-3, 0-8-0
875-899, Brooks, 1903,
rebuilt from F-9 2-8-0

Class H-4, 4-6-2
1441-1460, Baldwin, 1909
1461-1485, Lima, 1914

Class H-5, 4-6-2
1350-1374, GN, 1921-1927,
rebuilt from E-14 4-6-0

Class H-6, 4-6-2
1710-1724, GN, 1923,
rebuilt from J-1 and J-2 2-6-2

Class M-2, 2-6-8-0
1950-1984, GN, 1926-1928,
rebuilt from M-1 2-6-8-0, same numbers

Class N-3, 2-8-8-0
2000-2024, GN, 1940-1941,
rebuilt from N-2 2-8-8-0, same numbers

Class O-1, 2-8-2
3000-3144, Baldwin, 1911-1918

Class O-4, 2-8-2
3210-3254, Baldwin, 1920

Class O-6, 2-8-2
3350-3371, GN, 1925-1926,
Rebuilt from L-1 2-6-6-2

Class O-8, 2-8-2
3397-3399, GN, 1932
3375-3396, GN, 1945-1946,
rebuilt from O-7 2-8-2, same numbers

Class P-2, 4-8-2
2500-2527, Baldwin, 1923

Class Q-1, 2-10-2
2100-2129, Baldwin, 1923

Class Q-2, 2-10-2
2175-2189, GN, 1928,
rebuilt from P-1 4-8-2

Class R-2, 2-8-8-2
2044-2059, GN, 1929-1930

Class S-1, 4-8-4
2550-2555, Baldwin, 1929

Class S-2, 4-8-4
2575-2588, Baldwin, 1930

Class fireless 0-4-0, Sommers Lumber Co.
S-1 H.K. Porter, 1926
S-2 H.K. Porter, 1929

Source: *The Great Northern Railway Company: All-Time Locomotive Roster, 1861-1979*, Railroad History, Vol. 143 (Autumn 1980), reprinted by the Great Northern Railway Historical Society.

CLASS A 0-6-0

CLASS A • 6-WHEEL SWITCHER. Representing this class is No. 27, an A-9 with slide valves, Laird crossheads and Stephenson valve gear. Note the unusual driving wheel spacing and slope-backed tender with arch-bar trucks. Rogers built the first of GN's 0-6-0 yard goats in 1879, and hundreds of the breed from various builders were in use for the next 70 years. Small driving wheels provided high rail adhesion at limited speed, a desirable combination for yard work. Because of their small grate area, many of these locomotives burned coal and were hand-fired to operate on 160 pounds of saturated steam.

STEVE BOGEN

GN 53, A-9, 0-6-0, Series 1-94; 380-399
ABOVE • Built by Baldwin Locomotive Works (#31383) in July, 1907, GN 53 originally was equipped with 49" drivers, weighed 135,000 pounds and had a tractive effort of 26,050 pounds. The 53 was subsequently rebuilt with 52" drivers producing 26,850 pounds tractive effort. One of hundreds of 0-6-0's rostered by the GN over the years, note the number plate on the 53's smokebox door. Switching head-end equipment, the 53 is a survivor: by 1950 only a handful of 0-6-0's remained on the roster. The date of the photograph is 1949 and the 53 was scrapped in 1952.

CLASS C 0-8-0

CLASS C • 8-WHEEL SWITCHER. No. 818, a C-1, is representative of Great Northern's heaviest class of steam switcher. It had 19-inch piston valves, Walschaert valve gear, a Belpaire firebox and was oil-fired. The cab was bay window-equipped for winter service. Driving wheels were 55 inches in diameter, and 250 pounds of superheated steam drove the 26 x 28-inch cylinders. The reverse gear was of the Ragonnet type. GN's 0-8-0 switchers were purchased new from Baldwin in 1918. No. 818 was one of the last of these durable engines to be written off when steam operation was terminated on the GN in 1958.

CLASS C-1, 0-8-0, Series 810-49

LEFT • The class locomotive, GN 810 was built by Baldwin in June, 1918 (#48890). Equipped with 55" drivers, the 810 weighed 232,600 pounds and had a tractive effort of 58,500 pounds. Resting in the Kelly Lake, Minnesota roundhouse in July, 1956, the 810 remained on the roster until March, 1958 and was scrapped in 1962. Kelly Lake, centrally located on the Mesabi Range, was where ore jennies were assembled into trains and dispatched to the GN's iron ore classification yard at Allouez. The GN's heaviest class of steam switchers, Class C 0-8-0's were used on the Mesabi Range and at Allouez, not only to sort and classify iron ore but also to shove cuts of cars out onto the ore docks for unloading.

LLOYD KEYSER

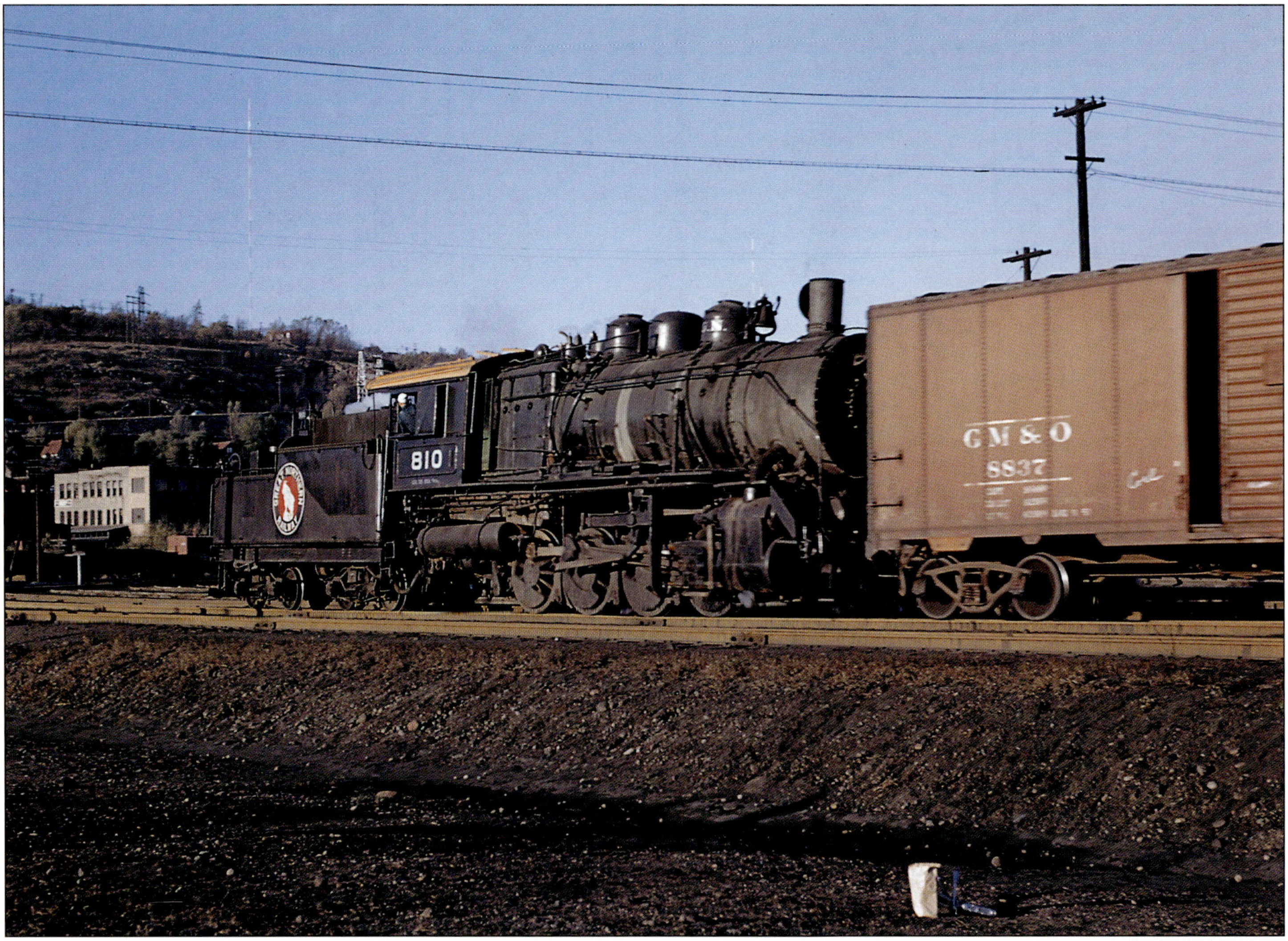

ROBERT F. COLLINS

GN 810

ABOVE • Doing the job for which it was designed, GN 810 pulls a cut of cars at Duluth on October 21, 1955. The engineer is leaning out the window to get a clear view. Note the 810's red roof and the large herald on the tender.

GN 823

BELOW • Easing off the turntable at Grand Forks, North Dakota on October, 4, 1957, GN 823 is readied for another day's work. All of the fifty C-1's remained on the roster until 1957 or 1958 and were active until the end of steam.

ROBERT F. COLLINS

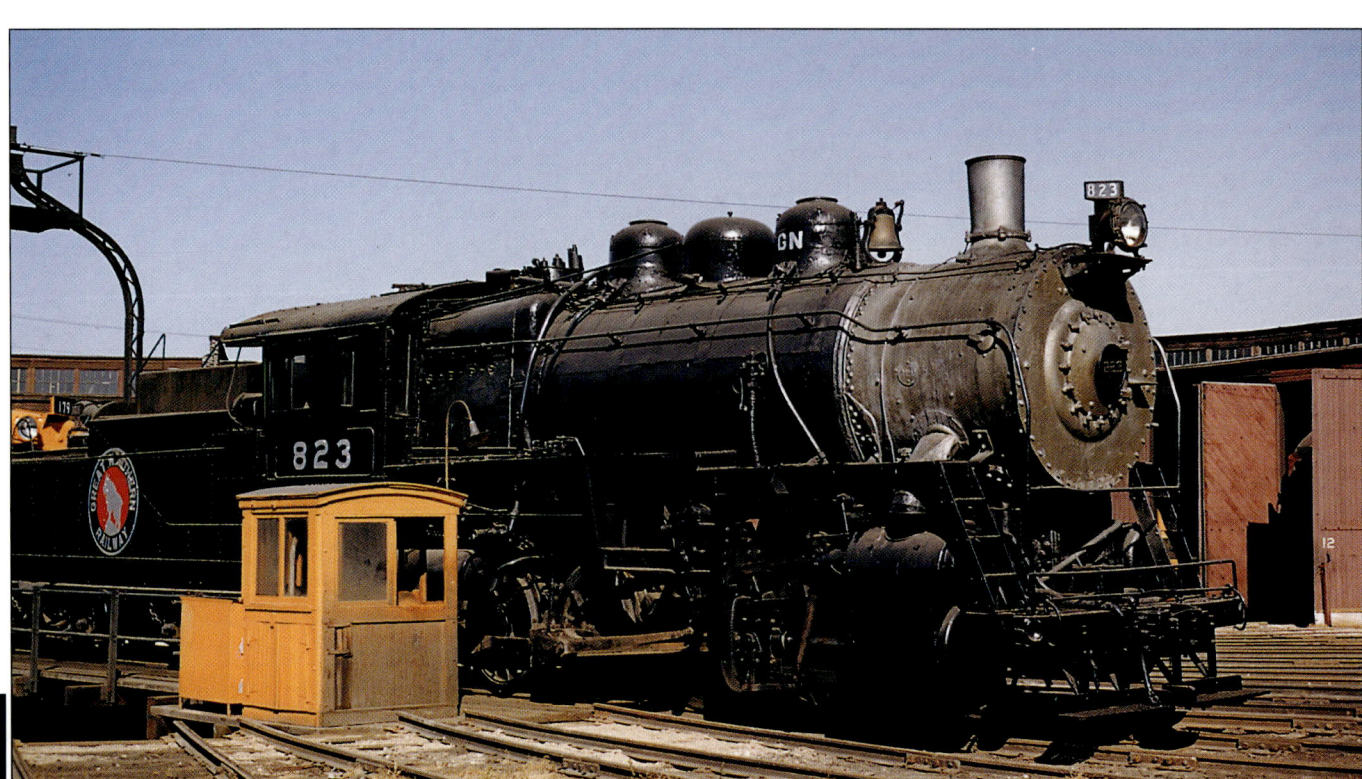

ROBERT F. COLLINS

GN 825
ABOVE • Steamed up and ready to work, GN 825 was photographed at Grand Forks on October 12, 1956. The C-1's were built by Baldwin in 1918 (810-831) and 1919 (832-849) and most provided the Great Northern with almost four decades of service.

GN 828
BELOW • Steaming quietly at a water pipe in Minneapolis on a warm August 18, 1956, GN 828 was built by Baldwin (#49658) in September, 1918. The 828 is beginning to show its age; retirement would come in December, 1957. Note the arch bar trucks on the 828's tender, common on GN switcher tenders even in the 1950's and not in violation of ICC regulations since the 828 and its mates were in yard service. That's a nice Chesapeake & Ohio 40' box car in the background.

JACK PFEIFER, ED AUSTIN COLLECTION

GN 832

ABOVE • Working at Minneapolis on October 13, 1956, the 832 was built by Baldwin (#51262) in February, 1919. With the engineer leaning out the bay window looking for a signal to back up, the 832 performs the job for which it was designed. Remaining on the roster until May, 1958, the 832 was scrapped in 1963. The C-1's were the Great Northern's primary heavy switcher, filling a need made evident during World War I and lasting until the end of steam.

GN 840

BELOW • In a marvelous picture which captures the essence of steam-era switching, GN 840 switches at Superior, Wisconsin on August 23, 1955. The fireman eyes the photographer warily while the man riding the footboards seems rather bemused by the situation. The 840 sports a brightly painted roof that seems several shades lighter than the mineral or oxide red that cab roofs were sometimes painted. The smokebox was painted silver although it has a nice covering of oil soot (all of the C-1's were oil burners). Note the Fruit Grower's Express wood reefer and the "tell-tale" which warned trainmen standing on a car roof of the impending overpass. The 840 remained on the roster until March, 1958 and was scrapped in 1962.

more Vital than gold

All the gold buried at Fort Knox, Ky., is less important to Victory than the rich iron ore deposits of the Mesabi, Cuyuna and Vermilion Ranges of Northern Minnesota.

The Mesabi range alone contains the world's largest developed deposits, and much of this ore lies in open pits.

From these pits giant shovels scoop the vital "red dust" into Great Northern cars, which dump it a few hours later into docks in Duluth and Superior, at the Head of the Lakes. There ore boats are swiftly loaded for delivery to the nation's steel mills.

When the shipping season closed December 5, new mining records had been set on the Minnesota ranges, and Great Northern Railway handled nearly 29,000,000 long tons — *a third of the Lake Superior district's total production.*

With the necessity of conserving equipment, Great Northern, between shipping seasons, is reconditioning motive power, cars, trackage, and its Allouez docks in Superior, making ready for a still bigger job in 1943.

The fabulous iron ore deposits in Minnesota are only part of the wealth contributed to America by the *Zone of Plenty* — and delivered by this vital artery of transportation.

GREAT NORTHERN RAILWAY
ROUTE OF THE EMPIRE BUILDER — BETWEEN THE GREAT LAKES AND THE PACIFIC

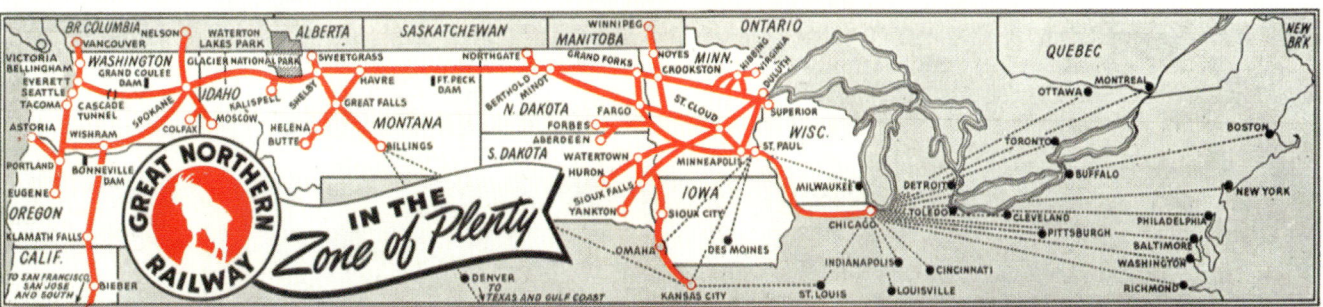

The extensive iron ore deposits of Minnesota's Mesabi Range were essential to the nation's war effort and the Great Northern hauled thousands upon thousands of ore jennies from the Mesabi Range to the Allouez docks in Superior, Wisconsin. The ore was mined primarily from open pits. Steam locomotives of the various mining companies hauled the ore out of the pits to an adjacent yard where the GN would collect the ore jennies and haul them to Kellys Lake and on to Allouez. Class C 0-8-0's were used to marshall the ore jennies at the yards and to push cuts of cars out onto the ore docks for unloading.

J. SCHMITT, ART PETERSON COLLECTION

GN 849
ABOVE • Having started with the first C-1 it is only appropriate that we include the 849, the last C-1 of the series, built by Baldwin in April, 1919 (#51671). The 849 is at an unknown location, probably Superior, Wisconsin, in the early 1950's. The Belpaire firebox became standard on GN steam locomotives in the 1890's and, with the exception of the P-2 and S-2 classes, all GN steam locomotives were equipped with this feature (as were locomotives of the Pennsylvania Railroad). The Belpaire featured a flat crown sheet with flat side and roof sheets which eliminated the need to use crown bars to support the crown sheet. The 849 remained on the roster until December, 1957 and was scrapped in 1962.

CLASS C-3, 0-8-0, Series 875-899
BELOW • After the C-1's were purchased from Baldwin, the remainder of the 0-8-0 fleet was rebuilt from 2-8-0's. GN 896 was rebuilt in 1927 from F-9 #1301. The C-3's had 55" drivers, 21" x 32" cylinders, an operating boiler pressure of 190 pounds, weighed 195,000 pounds and had a tractive effort of 41,440 pounds. The Great Northern had a rather frugal policy towards both rolling stock and locomotives and the GN's skilled shop personnel were quite adept at modifying or rebuilding steam locomotives to increase their utility. Posing with rods down at Seattle in 1949, the 896 has a silver smokebox and glossy light olive green boiler. The firebox appears to be a lighter shade of green. With the GN goat standing proudly on the tender's side, the 896 has been cared for with a great deal of pride.

STEVE BOGEN

CLASS H 4-6-2

CLASS H • PACIFIC. In 1926-27, Great Northern constructed a number of 4-6-2's from engines which originally were E-14 10-wheelers built by Baldwin in 1906. Boilers were lengthened by adding a combustion chamber, the firebox was widened and a Delta trailing truck applied. These redesigned locomotives, including No. 1369 (pictured here), joined GN's H-5 class. The handsome Pacific served Great Northern well for many years, powering such name trains as the Gopher, Alexandrian and, occasionally, the Oriental Limited. In later years these engines acquired Vanderbilt-type tenders, whose 12,000-gallon water and 5,800-gallon oil capacity permitted extended runs.

SANFORD GOODRICK

CLASS H-4, 4-6-2, Series 1441-1460
ABOVE • GN 1453, a Class H-4 4-6-2 was built by Baldwin in May, 1909 (BLW #33359). The H-4's were the first "modern" Pacifics on the Great Northern with Walschaerts valve gear, piston valves and Emerson superheaters. Riding on 73" drivers and weighing 235,750 pounds, the H-4's had 26" x 30" cylinders. Originally used in passenger service, the 1453 was in MOW service when photographed on September 5, 1950 at Scenic, Washington. With "LOOKOUT FOR OVERHEAD WIRES" stenciled on the rear of the tender, the 1354 was at home in the electrified district.

J. SCHMITT, ART PETERSON COLLECTION

**CLASS H-5, 4-6-2,
Series 1350-1374**

ABOVE • Over the years the Great Northern rostered 135 Pacifics in the H-1 to H-7 classes. After purchasing Pacifics from Rogers, Baldwin and Lima, the GN, starting with the H-5 Class, began to rebuild Class E-14 4-6-0's and Class J-1 and J-2 2-6-2's into 4-6-2's. The 1355 was rebuilt by the GN's Dale Street Shops in 1924 from Class E-14 1020 which was built by Baldwin (#33908) in 1909. Originally numbered 1494, it was renumbered 1355 in 1926. The 1355 had a long life on the Great Northern and spent its last years at Kelly Lake, Minnesota in Mesabi Division ore service, where it was photographed in the early 1950's. The 1355 was retired in 1955 and placed on display in Sioux City, Iowa. It is currently (1999) being restored to operating condition.

GN 1359

BELOW • Rebuilt by the GN's Dale Street Shops in 1924 from E-14 #1030, the 1359 was renumbered from GN 1495 in 1926. The 1359 had 23" x 30" cylinders and was equipped with Walschaert valve gear. Working boiler pressure was 200 psi, later increased to 210 psi. The 1359 weighed 260,800 pounds, of which 164,600 pounds were on the 73" drivers, resulting in a tractive effort of 38,580 pounds. Designed for passenger service, the 1359, in the company of the 1355 and 1369, spent its last years in iron ore service at Kelly Lake on the Mesabi Division, where it was photographed in the early 1950's.

J. SCHMITT, ART PETERSON COLLECTION

STEVE BOGEN

GN 1363
ABOVE • The H-5 Pacifics were assigned to passenger service across the system including, in 1924, the ORIENTAL LIMITED. Photographed in 1949 at Seattle, GN 1363 continues to perform its intended duty although it has been bumped from hauling the "varnish." Still wearing light olive on its boiler, the 1363 waits for its next assignment. Rebuilt by the Hillyard Shops from E-14 #1027 in 1926, the 1363 was scrapped in 1953.

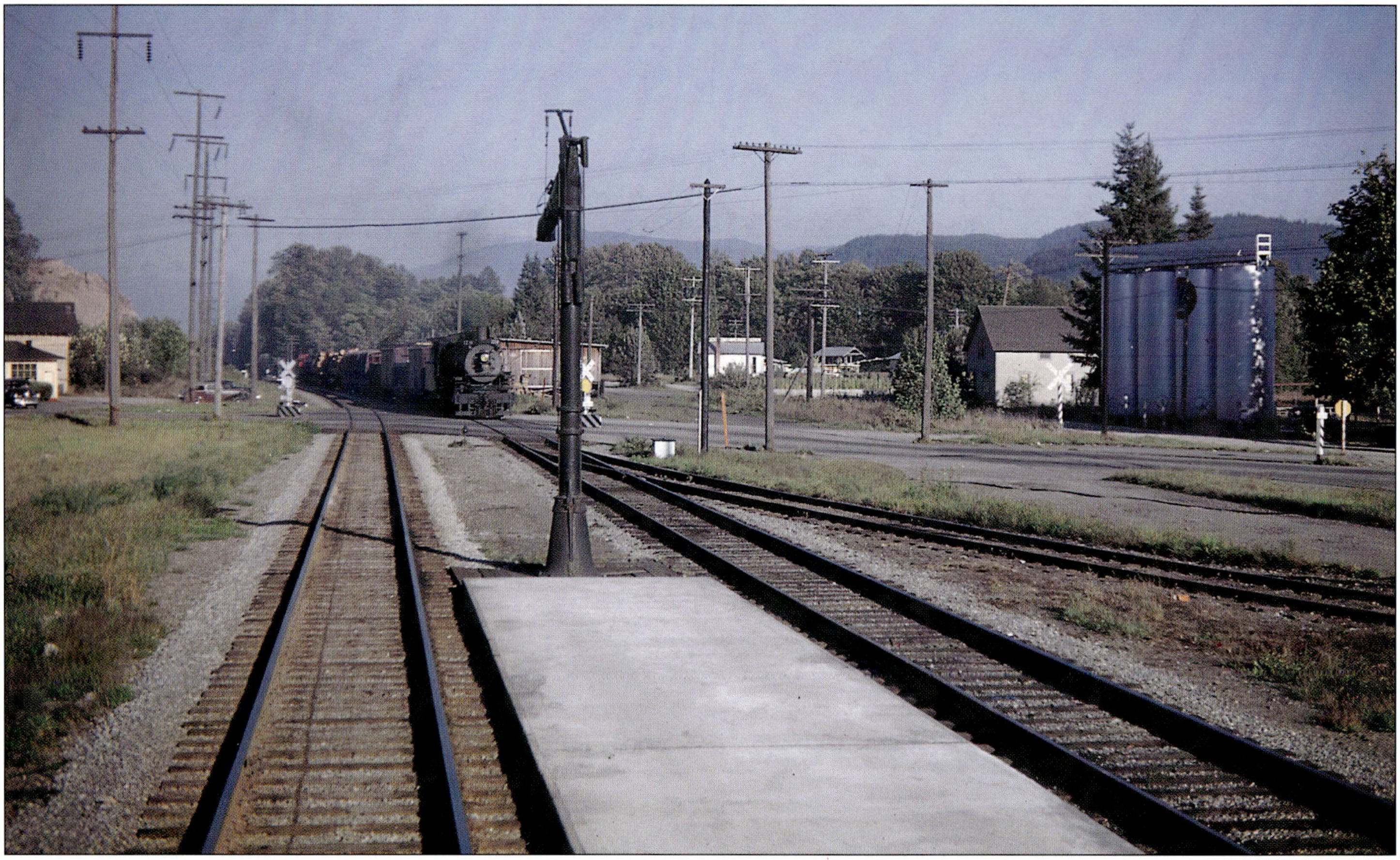

SANFORD GOODRICK

CLASS H-6, 4-6-2, Series 1710-1724

ABOVE & BELOW • Class H-6 Pacifics were rebuilt from J-1 and J-2 2-6-2's by the Dale Street Shops in a program that started in 1921 and ended in 1927. The 1710 was the program's first graduate, rebuilt from GN 1710 in 1921. Riding on 69" drivers, the 1710 had a tractive effort of 40,810 pounds. In these two photographs, the 1710 is at Index, Washington with a local freight on September 5, 1950. Uncoupling from its train at a road crossing, the 1710 and a car to be dropped off pull up to the water spout for a drink while the brakeman guards the crossing. Sandy Goodrick photographed the action from the rear of the CASCADIAN.

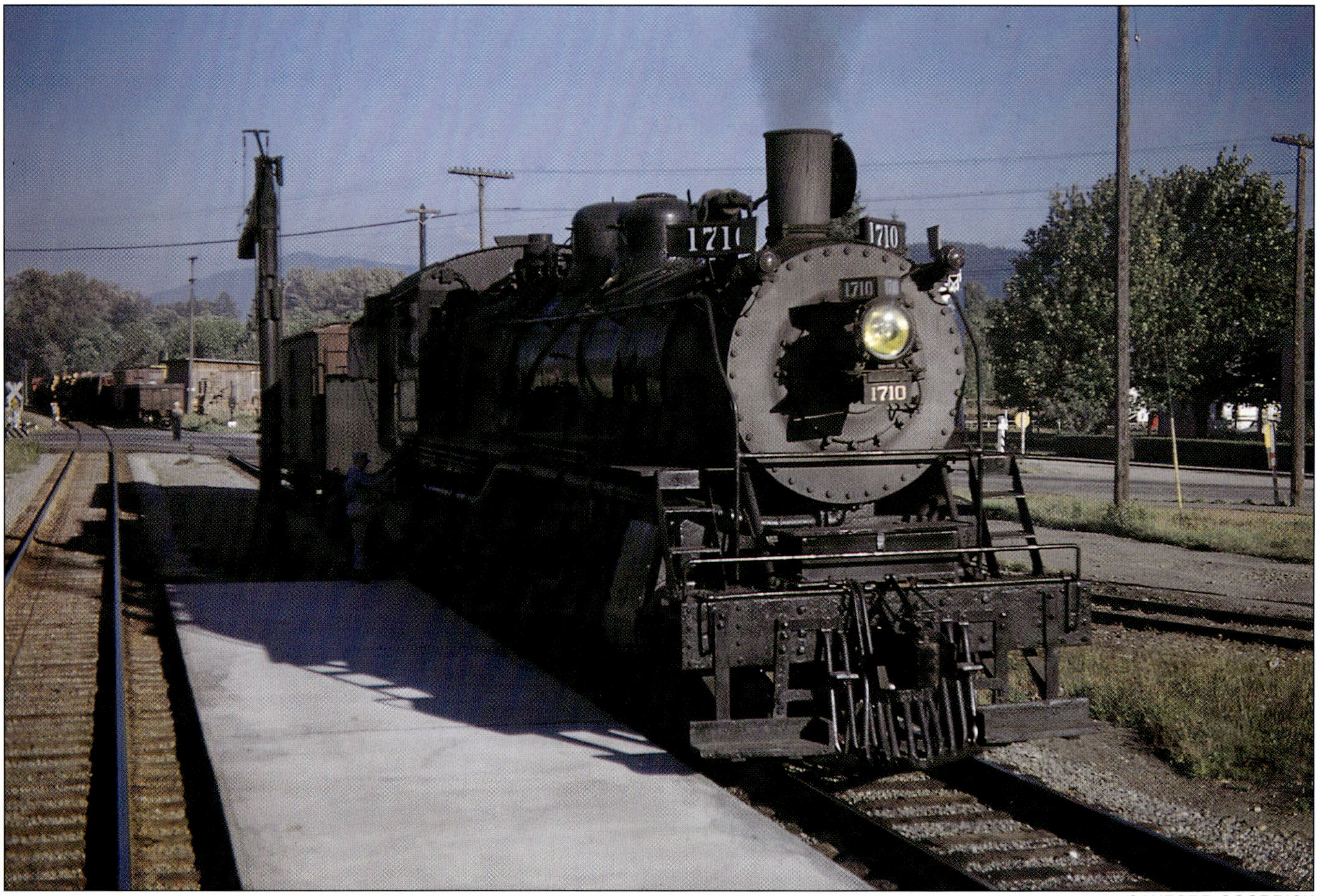

SANFORD GOODRICK

CLASS M 2-6-8-0

CLASS M • MALLET-ARTICULATED. Another true Mallet type as originally constructed by Baldwin in 1910 was Great Northern's M class 2-6-8-0, a compound with 23/35 x 32-inch cylinders. In 1926–27 these M-1 engines were rebuilt by GN as simple articulated M-2's, having 22/23½ x 32-inch cylinders. Weight was approximately 201 tons and drivers were of 55-inch diameter. (An example is No. 1973, shown here.) The M-2 had a relatively short life, for these engines were destined to be rebuilt again by the GN in 1929–31 as O-7's (2-8-2). Finally, between 1944–46, most of the O-7's were converted to O-8's.

J. SCHMITT, ART PETERSON COLLECTION

CLASS M-2, 2-6-8-0, Series 1950-1984
ABOVE • In December, 1909 and in 1910 the Great Northern received thirty 2-6-8-0's that looked like, in the words of one GN author, a shotgun marriage of a mogul and a 0-8-0 switcher. These behemoths were rebuilt by GN shops in 1926 and 1927 as M-2's. The rebuilt simple articulated locomotives had 55" drivers and weighed 403,000 pounds. The drivers supported 384,000 pounds for a tractive effort of 95,500 pounds. These locomotives were pullers and both the original Baldwins and rebuilt versions found a home on the Iron Range. Many of the rebuilt M-2's had short lives as beginning in 1929 they were rebuilt into Class O-7 2-8-2's. The 1977 was one of thirteen M-2's to escape the rebuilding program, and remained on the roster until 1954. Photographed on an unknown date at Kelly Lake, Minnesota, the 1977 shows the effects of almost three decades of heavy tonnage service.

CLASS N 2-8-8-0

CLASS N · MALLET-ARTICULATED. The N class (2-8-8-0) engines originated with Baldwin in 1912, and were Mallet type (compound) having 28/42 x 32-inch cylinders. They operated on 210 pounds of superheated steam and weighed 225 tons. During 1925-27 the original N-1's, 25 in all, were made into simple articulated engines, modernized and reclassified as N-2's (see photo of No. 2000). In 1940-41 new nickel steel boilers were applied, along with roller bearings and other modern features. Operating steam power was upped to 265 pounds, cylinders were 22/22 x 32-inches and weight of the engine was increased to 286 tons.

GN 2020

ABOVE • The story of Great Northern's N-3's begins in 1912 when Baldwin built 25 2-8-8-0's numbered 2000 through 2024. These locomotives, classified N-1, weighed approximately 450,000 pounds (640,000 pounds with tender) with 420,000 pounds on the drivers resulting in a tractive effort of 93,250 pounds. Built as compound articulates with high pressure rear cylinders (28" x 32") and low pressure front cylinders (42" x 32"), the 2000-2016 burned coal and the 2017-2024 were oil burners. From 1924-1927 the N-1's were rebuilt into simple articulates with all four cylinders measuring 25" x 32". In 1939 the tractive effort increased to 100,000 pounds, the locomotives were reclassified as N-2's. In 1940 the GN initiated another rebuilding program, installing new nickel-steel boilers built by Baldwin, cast steel engine beds from General Steel Casting and Timken roller bearings. The 2020 received a semi-streamlined cab and Sellers exhaust steam injectors. Classified N-3, the cylinders were 22" x 32" and the tractive effort was 118,400 pounds. Many of the N-3's remained active until the end of steam and were retired between 1955 and 1957. The N-3's were a mainstay on the Mesabi Division where the 2020 was photographed on an unknown date. The low sun angle provides an excellent view of the 2020 and its Vanderbilt tender.

J. SCHMIT, ART PETERSON COLLECTION

GAYLE CHRISTEN

CLASS N-3, 2-8-8-0, Series 2000-2024

ABOVE • In one of the more spectacular color photographs of a Great Northern steam locomotive that the author has seen, GN 2012 steams at the Hillyard Shops in September, 1951. Just released from the paint shop, the 2012 provides us with an excellent example of how GN steam locomotives were painted in the early 1950's. The boiler, cylinder saddles and air pumps are light olive green, and the smokebox and firebox are painted with a mixture of white and silver. The rest of the 2012, to include the cab roof, is black. Red cab roofs, characteristic of what is called the "Glacier Park" paint scheme, and used especially on the Kalispell Division, were never part of an official Great Northern paint scheme.

21

Great Northern Railway Co.
65th Annual Report
1953

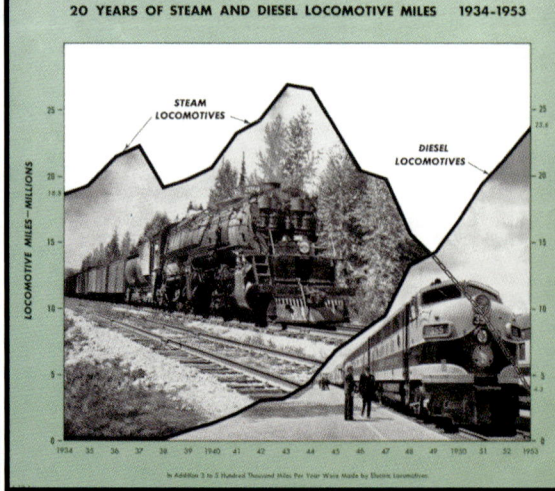

In common with other railroads of the 1950s, the GN felt obliged to show its dieselization progress to its stockholders in its 1953 Annual Report.

CLASS O 2-8-2

CLASS O . MIKADO. The popular Mikado (2-8-2) was best exemplified on Great Northern by the celebrated 0-8. The first three engines in this sub-class (3397-3399) were GN-built in 1932, and were the only locomotives constructed in the U. S. that year for domestic service. The 0-8 was not only the heaviest Mikado type ever built, but the heaviest on axle of any steam locomotive, aggregating 81,250 pounds per axle. Originally designed steam pressure was 280 pounds, but this was later reduced to 250 pounds. Twenty-two rebuilt 0-7's joined the 0-8 class in 1944–46.

SANFORD GOODRICK

CLASS 0-1, 2-8-2, Series 3070-3144
ABOVE • The Mikado was one of the most important and numerous steam locomotives on the Great Northern: between 1911 and 1919 Baldwin delivered 145 2-8-2's. By 1942 the GN rostered 264 Mikes in classes 0-1 to 0-8, 33% of the GN roster. GN 3089, at Sauk Centre, Minnesota on May 25, 1953, was built by Baldwin (#44203) in 1916. The 3089 had 63" drivers, a total weight of 306,500 pounds, with 229,000 pounds resting on the drivers resulting in a tractive effort of 60,930 pounds. Cylinders were 28" x 32" with an operating steam pressure of 180 pounds. Originally equipped with a Street Stoker and Franklin grate shakers (many of the 0-1's were later converted to oil burners and the stokers were removed) the 0-1's had Walschaert valve gear. Setting out and picking up cars at Sauk Centre, we get an excellent view of the Great Northern right-of-way, to include small buildings, the pole line, and, in the distance, a water tank and grain elevator. Note the fuel truck to the left of the 3089.

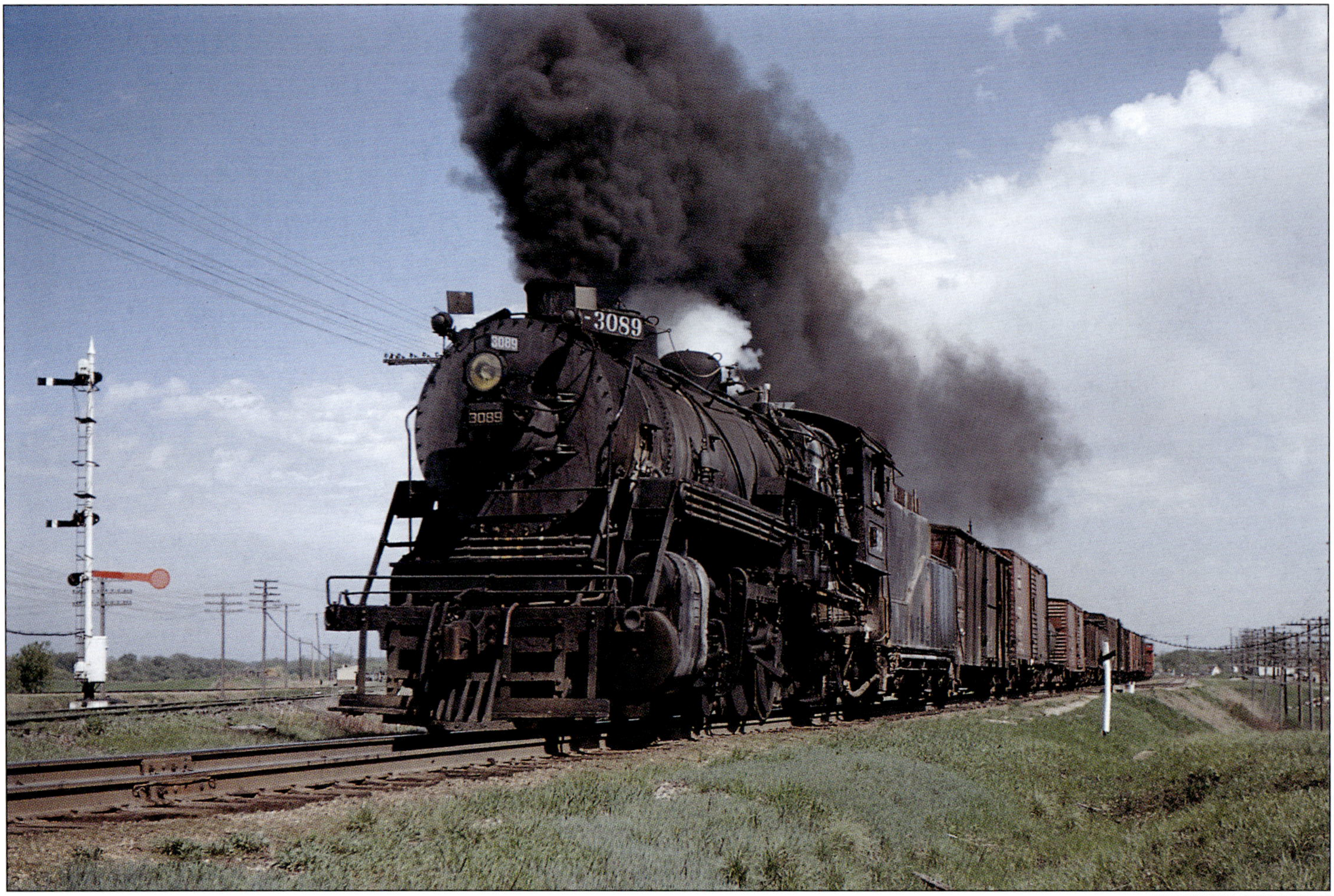

SANFORD GOODRICK

GN 3089

ABOVE • Sandy Goodrick provides us with two more views of the 3089 on a beautiful May 25, 1953. The 3089 departs Sauk Centre with a nice plume of smoke and about ten cars. Its consist includes wood and steel box cars, two hoppers, a tank car and, of course, a bright red caboose. While we can't see the detail of the consist, note that the box cars are all painted with variations of mineral, or box car, red. Brightly colored box cars were not a part of day-to-day railroading on the Great Northern in 1953.

GN 3089

BELOW • After departing Sauk Centre, the 3089 was also photographed east of Osakis, Minnesota with a Milwaukee outside-braced box car and a Frisco box car in tow. Sauk Centre and Osakis were located west of St. Cloud, Minnesota and were 116 and 130 miles, respectively, west of St. Paul.

SANFORD GOODRICK

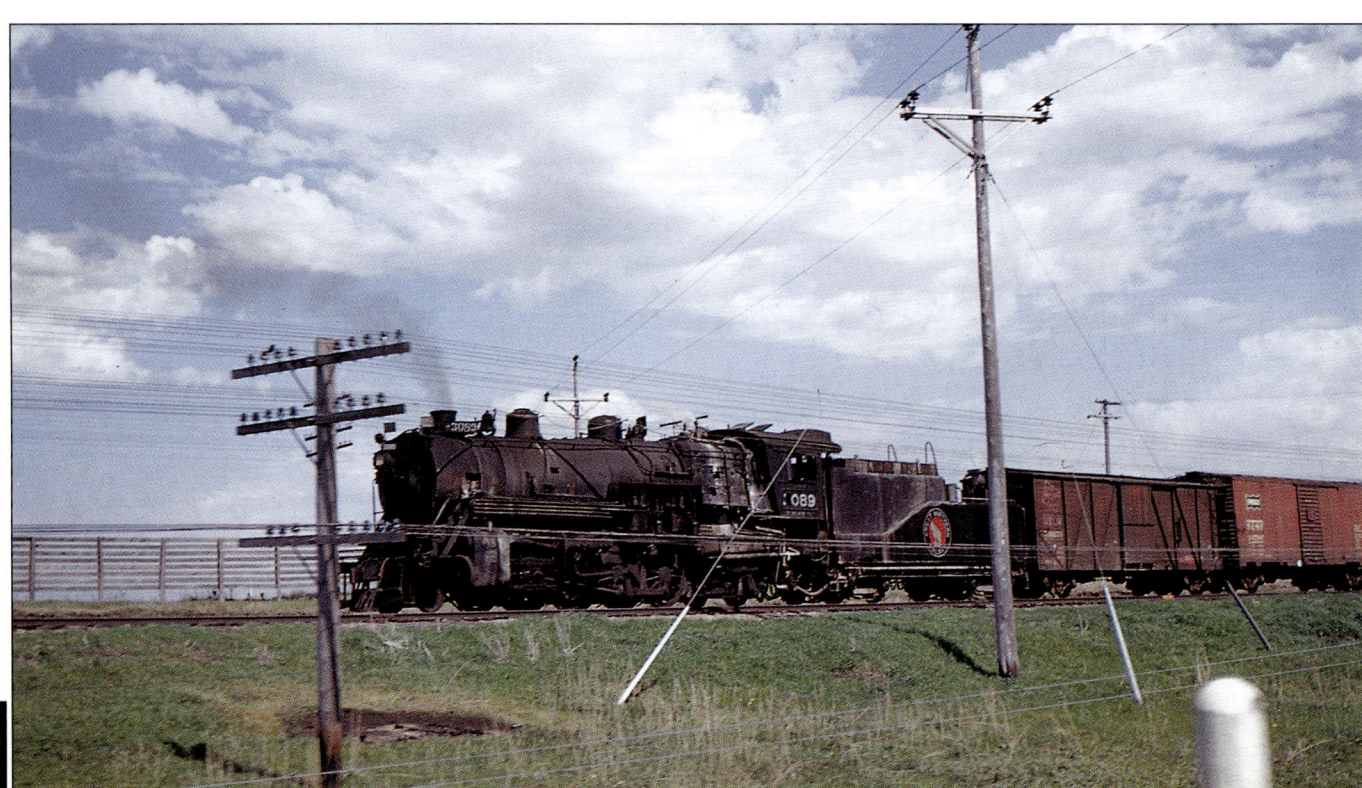

J. J. BUCKLEY

GN 3100
ABOVE • Built by Baldwin in 1917 (#46213) GN 3100 rests at Kelly Lake, Minnesota on an unknown date. In the 1940's the 3100, along with the 3071, 3106, 3135, 3137, 3138, 3142, 3144 were equipped with Delta trailing trucks with a booster rated between 11,000 and 12,000 pounds. These boosters were removed by the early 1950's. The O-1's were originally delivered with tenders having a capacity of 13 tons of coal and 8,000 gallons of water. The tenders were modified or rebuilt over the years resulting in greater capacity. Over its lifespan an O-1 may have had as many as four different tenders. The 3100's last tender was a Class P-2, style 104 Vanderbilt tender, #2507.

GN 3125
BELOW • Assigned to ballast train service when photographed at Cloquet, Minnesota in 1954, GN 3125 was built by Baldwin (#49356) in 1918. Pushing a wood dozer and an ore jenny converted to ballast service, the 3125 has been outfitted with an auxiliary tender, extending the time it can work before having to find a water tank. Cloquet is located 39 miles west of Duluth on the line to Grand Rapids, Bemidji and Crookston, Minnesota.

CARL HEHL, LOU SCHMITZ COLLECTION

STEVE BOGEN

STEVE BOGEN

ROBERT F. COLLINS

CLASS O-4, 2-8-2, Series 3210-3254

PREVIOUS PAGE, ABOVE & BELOW • In 1920 Baldwin built forty-five Mikados for the Great Northern. These locomotives, designated O-4, weighed 319,700 pounds with 242,800 pounds on the drivers. Heavier than the O-1's, tractive effort was 64,310 pounds compared to the O-1's 60,930 pounds. The O-4's had 63" drivers, 28" x 32" cylinders and an operating pressure of 190 pounds. In the Seattle area in 1949, the 3216 (Baldwin #53837) takes on water and then continues its journey. With light olive green adorning the boiler, cylinder jackets and pumps, the 3216 looks pretty sharp as it goes about its business.

GN 3216

ABOVE • By 1957 the 3216 had moved east to Grand Forks where Bob Collins photographed it on October 4, 1957. Posing in the sun with its Vanderbilt tender, the 3216 has a far more utilitarian look to it than when we last saw it in Seattle in 1949. Note the tank cars on the adjacent track which are in fuel oil service, supplying the fuel necessary to keep the Great Northern's fleet of oil burners on the move.

LEFT • There is no argument that Glacier National Park is one of the most spectacular scenic areas in the United States. The Great Northern realized the significance of the area quite early and played an instrumental role in the establishment of Glacier National Park and its subsequent development as a place in which to spend one's summer vacation. Hotels, chalets, roads and trails were built by the GN. Vacationers would, of course, arrive in Glacier by train and stay in company hotels. This pre-World War II ad (1941) shows the unique observation motor coaches which the Glacier Park Hotel Company (incorporated in 1914 as a subsidiary company of the Great Northern) provided tours of the Park. Today, one can still take tours in these coaches although the railroad no longer owns the hotel company.

GN 3224

With a bright red caboose on tow, the 3224 is ready for a day's work. In Minneapolis on August 21, 1955, the 3224 was built in 1920 (Baldwin #53984). With its 64,310 pounds of tractive effort, the O-4's earned their keep in a variety of assignments.

JACK PFEIFER, ED AUSTIN COLLECTION

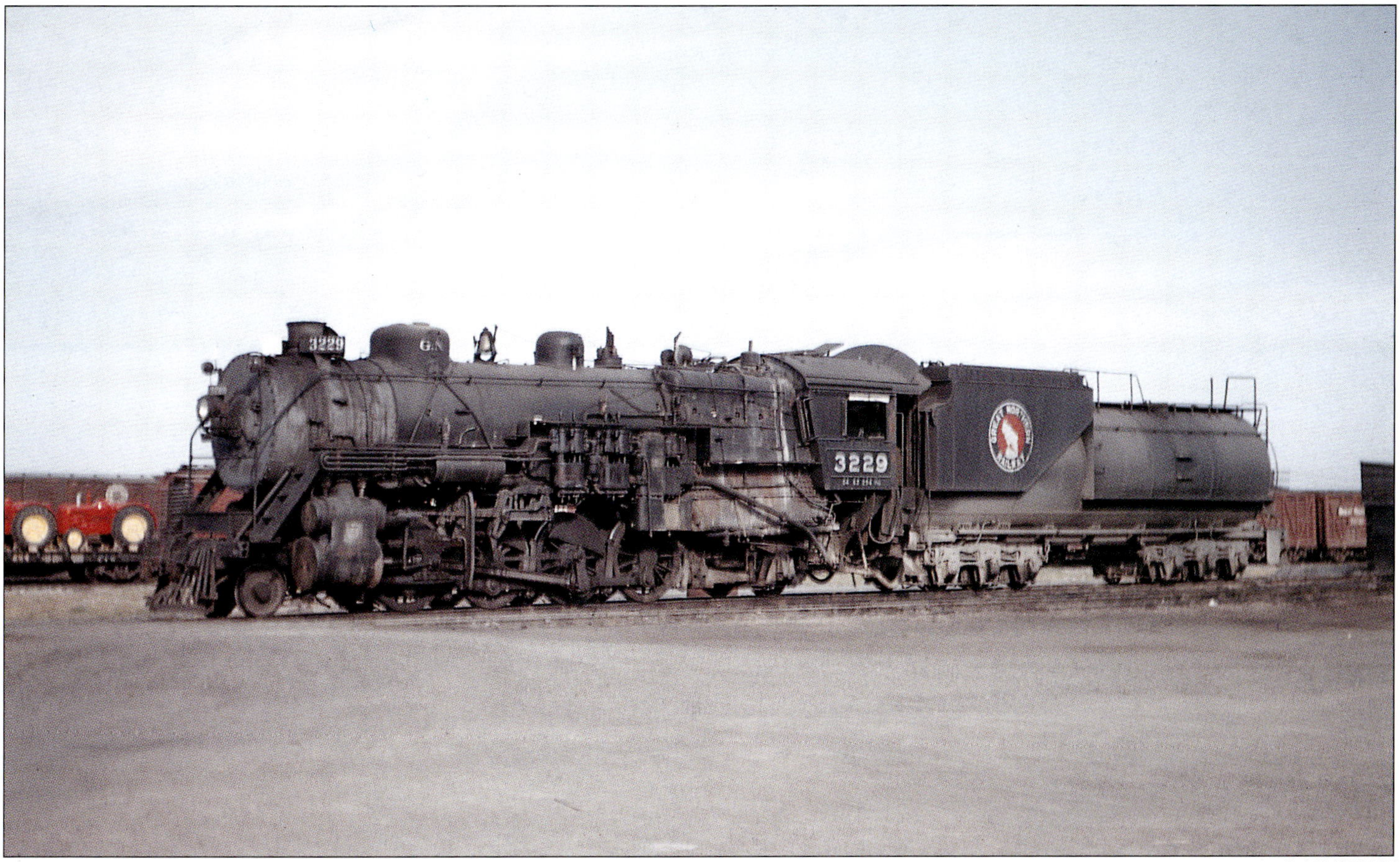

J. J.BUCKLEY

GN 3229 and 3233

ABOVE & BELOW • Two O-4's, the 3229 (Baldwin #54029) and 3233 (Baldwin #54033) pose for comparison photos at the same location on an unknown date. Nearing the end of active service (the 3229 was retired in 1957 and scrapped in 1962 and the 3233 was scrapped in 1956) the two Mikes show the wear, tear and lack of maintenance that characterized the last days of steam. Comparison of the two locomotives shows that over the years numerous shopping resulted in minor differences from locomotive to locomotive so no two are alike. Note, for example, the difference in the size of the air reservoir, and the arrangement of water pipes and pumps.

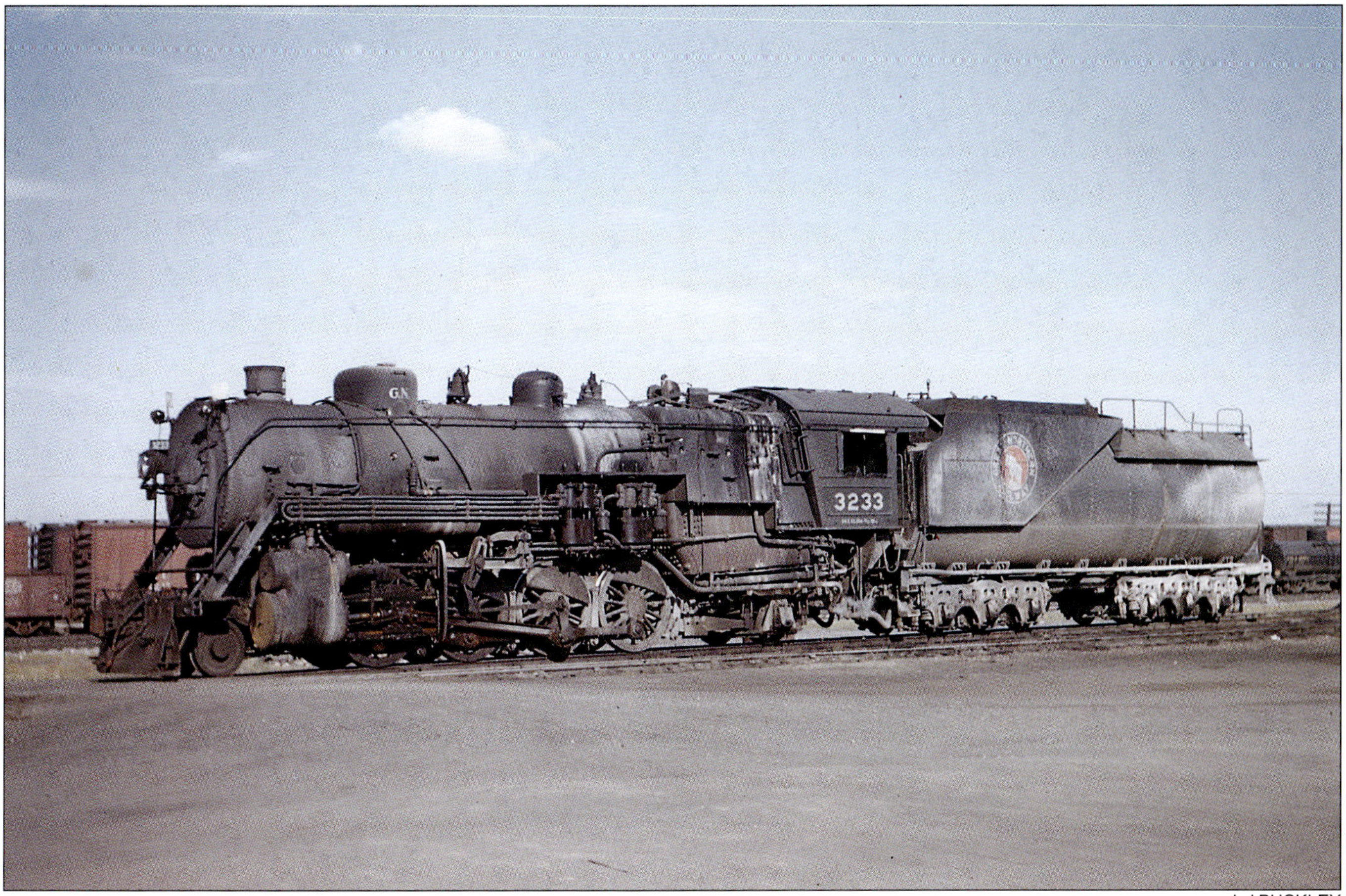

J. J.BUCKLEY

JACK PFEIFER, ED AUSTIN COLLECTION

JACK PFEIFER, ED AUSTIN COLLECTION

JACK PFEIFER, ED AUSTIN COLLECTION

GN Class O-6, 2-8-2, Series 3350-3371

PREVIOUS PAGE, TOP • In January, 1922 the Great Northern began its first massive building program, converting 45 L-2 Mallets into O-5 Mikados. The success of this program led to another rebuilding: 22 L-1 2-6-6-2's were rebuilt in GN shops, emerging as Class O-6 2-8-2's. The O-6's weighed 320,100 pounds with 244,000 pounds on the drivers, producing a tractive effort of 66,000 pounds. The O-6's cylinders were 28" x 32" and operating steam pressure was 195 pounds. The drivers were 63" in diameter, increased from 53" by taking 4" steel bands and shrinking them over the old wheel centers and applying new tires.

PREVIOUS PAGE, BOTTOM • Jack Pfeifer visited Willmar, Minnesota on November 8, 1953, and photographed eastbound GN 3358 entering and leaving Willmar. Seen above, the 3358 swings onto the yard lead with 72 cars in tow, including a reefer next to the tender and a cut of livestock cars. The 3358 was rebuilt from L-1 #1903 by GN's Delta Shops in Everett, Washington and was completed in January, 1903. In a going away shot, the 3358 passes the scales. Note the detail of the wood reefer. The 3358 was constructed as an oil burner as were all O-6's. The O-6's were originally assigned rectangular tenders with a capacity of 4,500 gallons of oil and 8,000 gallons of water. The tender capacities were later increased to carry 10,000 gallons of water. The 3358 in 1933 was assigned Class R-1, Style 108 tender #2040. Most of the O-6's were later assigned Style 112 Vanderbilt tenders, the first of which were purchased separately by the GN and assigned to individual numbers. The 3358 was assigned Style 112 tender #2091 which it kept for the remainder of its service.

ABOVE • In Willmar the 3358 set off and picked up cars, leaving Willmar eastbound with 90 cars, most of them tank cars. As it departs Willmar the 3358 passes the Western Fruit Express icehouse. Note the ice on the icing platform. Willmar was a crew change point and with lines to St. Cloud, Sioux Falls, South Dakota and the main to Fargo, North Dakota, it was a hub of activity.

RIGHT • In this photo, the 3358 crosses over to the eastbound main. Both photographs provide a good view of the signals and associated equipment required for the crossovers.

JACK PFEIFER, ED AUSTIN COLLECTION

LEFT • Departing, the 3358 exhausts a magnificent plume of smoke as it attacks the grade east of Willmar.

JACK PFEIFER, ED AUSTIN COLLECTION

GN Class O-8, 2-8-2, Series 3397-3399; 3375-3396

BELOW • While the O-1 to O-6 Mikes served the Great Northern well, the GN's motive power department was interested in obtaining more speed from their Mikes. Accordingly, authorization was obtained to build twenty-five 2-8-2's from M-2 Class 2-6-8-0's. From 1929 to 1932 twenty-two M-2's were rebuilt into Class O-7 2-8-2's in the GN's Superior, Great Falls, and Hillyard Shops. The boilers from the L-1's and L-2's had been used in the O-5 and O-6 rebuilds, new 69" drivers were purchased for the O-7's. The larger drivers allowed increased speed and better balancing of the large piston thrust. The O-7's weighed 348,000 pounds with 268,000 pounds on the drivers. The cylinders measured 31" x 32" and operating steam pressure was 210 pounds. The O-7's were substantially heavier than the earlier classes of Mikes and had 79,550 pounds tractive effort. Although faster, the O-7's were slippery and the boilers did not steam as well as anticipated. The O-7's also had frequent problems with broken cylinders, loosened cylinders, sheared and loosened frame bolts and working guides. This would eventually lead to a new design, Class O-8, and all 22 O-7's would be rebuilt into O-8's. The O-8 originated with a decision to redesign the last three O-7's. In 1932 the Hillyard Shops began construction of what was to become the heaviest Mikes ever built. The GN purchased new boilers from Baldwin rather than reuse boilers from the articulates. Similar to the boilers on the S-1 Northerns, they had a much larger Belpaire firebox. Conventional wisdom would have a four wheel truck on a locomotive as large as the O-8, but the GN utilized two-wheeled Delta trucks in order to significantly increase the weight on the drivers. The first three O-8's weighed 367,000 pounds with 280,000 pounds on the drivers. Tractive effort was 78,000 pounds. The Great Northern was well pleased with its three O-8's but the Great Depression precluded any further construction.

GN 3399 takes on water in Minneapolis on August 21, 1955. One of the three original O-8's, it was built by the Hillyard Shops in 1932. In 1946 the 3397, 3398 and 3399 were shopped at Superior and rebuilt to the same standards as the 3375-3396. This view of the 3399 gives an indication of the O-8's strength. Just looking at the locomotive one can tell that it means business; a no nonsense, no frills locomotive in line with Jim Hill's philosophy of maximizing ton mileage with minimum train mileage. The 3399, along with the 3397 and 3398, were true pioneers in the development of Great Northern steam. Taking on water, the 3399 looks as if it is just another steam locomotive, near the end of its service, doing its day-to-day duty. Jim Hill would be proud.

JACK PFEIFER, LOU SCHMITZ COLLECTION

JACK PFEIFER, ED AUSTIN COLLECTION

GN 3377

ABOVE • World War II brought record levels of traffic to the Great Northern. The GN had an urgent need for additional motive power to meet wartime demands. Diesels were the first choice: in 1941 nine EMD FT units were received and four more were delivered in 1943. Additional units were on order but with the War Production Board allocating new motive power, diesels were not forthcoming. In 1943 the GN decided to rebuild the O-7's into O-8's in order to increase performance. Delivered from 1944-1946, the 22 locomotives retained their old numbers. Converted to oil burners (most of the O-7's were coal burners), the O-8's were converted by the Superior shops except for the 3388 and 3394 which were rebuilt at Great Falls. With new boilers from Baldwin and Alco, total weight increased to 425,540 pounds with 325,000 pounds riding on the drivers. Cylinders were 28" x 32". Tractive effort was a whopping 78,000 pounds; thus the O-8's were the most powerful class of Mikes built anywhere in the world. This pulling ability mounted on 69" drivers resulted in a speed capability more typical of a 4-8-4. Indeed, although the GN's S-1 and S-2 Northerns were faster and more efficient at evaporating water, the 0-8 was more efficient in that on a ton-mile basis, it hauled the most tonnage using the least amount of fuel and water. With the O-8's the Great Northern had created perhaps their most outstanding locomotive. O-8's were heavier, and had more tractive effort and horsepower than any other Mikado, as well as many Berkshires and some Northerns. Noted railroad author David P. Morgan called the O-8's "Berkshires on a Mikado frame, and then some." Morgan further noted that the O-8's could start a heavier train than most Berkshires and could "run with the best of them". The photographs that follow offer visual testimony to Morgan's claims. The Great Northern shops had built a truly outstanding locomotive.

On November 7, 1953, Jack Pfeifer Photographed GN 3377 being serviced at Willmar. The 3377 was built by the GN's Great Falls shop in 1933 from M-2 #1978 and converted to an O-8 in 1945 by the GN's Superior, Wisconsin shops. The O-8's were originally painted in the olive jacket scheme. However, on October 6, 1950 the shops were directed to paint all O-8's black, hence the black-boilered 3377 seen here.

RIGHT • As active as the Great Northern was in promoting Glacier National Park, it must have been painful for the GN to close their hotels and chalets in the park during World War II. To keep the park in the minds of the public the Great Northern ran ads such as this featuring a lonesome Rocky with tears in his eyes. Was this the only time that Rocky was pictured crying?

JACK PFEIFER, ED AUSTIN COLLECTION

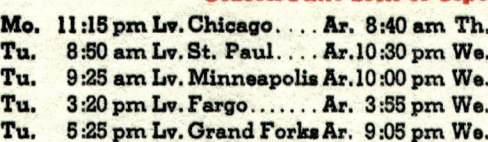

JACK PFEIFER, ED AUSTIN COLLECTION

PRECEDING PAGE & ABOVE• The next day, November 7, 1953, Jack photographed the 3377 departing Willmar westbound with 119 cars. Thundering out of the yard onto the westbound main, the 3377 creates a magnificent plume of steam and smoke. It is no wonder that railfans of the early 1940's found diesels to be a poor substitute for steam! Both the locomotives and tenders had Timken roller bearings on all journals, and GN engineers agreed that the O-8's were fast starters. It was said that O-8's could get a train moving faster than any other type of steam locomotive on the Great Northern. On the Willmar Division speeds of 60 mph with 4500 tons (approximately 75 cars) were common and the O-8's could move 6500 tons (about 125 cars) at 45 mph. Looking at the 3377 departing Willmar, there is no reason to doubt those figures!

GAYLE CHRISTEN

GN 3376
ABOVE • GN 3376 sits in the sun outside the Hillyard Shops on August 27, 1952. The 3376 was built by the Superior Shops in 1945 from O-7 #3376 which, in turn, was built at the Hillyard Shops in 1930 from M-2 #1978. While the aesthetics of steam locomotives is highly subjective, the O-8's are considered by many to be the handsomest heavy Mikado to roll the rails. The 3376 lived out its last days assigned to the Mesabi Division using its steam to thaw frozen ore.

GN 3379
BELOW • In Minneapolis on August 15, 1956 and with a caboose for company, GN 3379 has stopped for water before heading off to complete its daily chores. Built at Superior in 1946 using an Alco boiler, the 3379 was originally built as an O-7 at Great Falls in 1930 from M-2 #1962. The O-8's were popular with engineers, not just for their pulling power and speed, but also because the heavy weight on the drivers meant a higher rate of pay.

LOU SCHMITZ

LOU SCHMITZ

GN 3381

ABOVE • GN 3381 works a westbound in Minneapolis on August 21, 1955 in the company of Class O-4 2-8-2 #3224. Built by the Superior Shops in 1946 from an O-7 of the same number, its lineage can be traced back to M-2 #1954. Note the absence of colorful freight cars in this mid-1950 scene. Before covered hoppers became prevalent, 40' box cars were used to haul grain. The Illinois Central box car to the left of the 3381 was in grain service as evidenced by the plywood sheeting covering the door opening.

BELOW • Making its presence known as its storms by the Honeywell building Minneapolis on August 10, 1955, an unidentified Great Northern Mike leaves Union Yard with an impressive plume of smoke and, undoubtedly, a considerable amount of stack talk. The 40' box car reigns supreme in this scene. Not only are several different railroads represented, but note also the variety in construction techniques, height, etc.

BOB WANNER

GN 3390

BELOW & RIGHT • On a sunny October 14, 1956, GN O-8 #3390 powered a freight from St. Paul, Minnesota west to Willmar. J.J. Buckley paced the 3390 as it went about its chores on this beautiful fall day. We see the 3390 first in St. Paul with a caboose enroute to pick up its train. With a long train of box cars, the 3390 was next photographed leaving Minneapolis with metal white flags indicating its status as an extra freight. Prototype modelers would do well to study the 3390's consist: 40' box cars from several railroads, and considerable variety in construction, height and shades of box car red. Many of the doors are open indicating a healthy load of empties heading west.

J. J. BUCKLEY

ABOVE • Jim Hill cast an eye towards Asia long before the Great Northern reached Seattle. Following World War II GN management was interested in resuming trade with Asia as a means to stimulate traffic in the post World War II era.

J. J. BUCKLEY

ABOVE • The 3390 rounds the curve at Wayzata, 24 miles west of St. Paul.

BELOW • Further west, the 3390 storms past the Maple Plain depot (31 miles west of St. Paul). The upper quadrant train order semaphore indicates clear. An everyday scene on the Great Northern in the 1950's, how many of us wish we could have been standing on the depot platform to watch the 3390 thunder by?

J. J. BUCKLEY

J. J. BUCKLEY

ABOVE • Pacing the 3390 on US 12, J.J. Buckley's last shot is from the depot in Montrose, Minnesota, 14 miles west of Maple Plain and 45 miles west of St. Paul. Note the standard GN platform light. It looks like the corn in the background is ready to harvest. Garrison Keillor's fictional Lake Woebegone (pop. 492) was served by a Great Northern branchline and this scene is similar to descriptions of Lake Woebegone ("...the municipal boundaries take in quite a bit of pasture and cropland, including wheat, corn and alfalfa..." Also, "the view is spoiled somewhat by a large grain elevator by the railroad track.").

J. J. BUCKLEY

JACK PFEIFER, ED AUSTIN COLLECTION

GN 3391

ABOVE & BELOW • GN 3391 steams impatiently at Willmar, Minnesota on November 7, 1953. Judging from the smoke, a stiff wind is blowing. Winds on the Dakota prairie were at times strong enough that an engineer had to work steam downhill in order to keep the train moving. This was the primary reason that Mikados were the exception rather than the rule between Minot and Williston, North Dakota. With 40' box cars extending out of sight, the 3391 has enlisted help from SW-9 #20, purchased from EMD in 1951.

JACK PFEIFER, ED AUSTIN COLLECTION

J. J. BUCKLEY

GN 3394

ABOVE • This view of a Great Northern O-8 is quite symbolic: On a dark and cloudy October 13, 1956 in St. Paul, O-8 3394 is surrounded by EMD FT's. Although the 3394 will extend its life by providing steam to thaw frozen iron ore on the Mesabi Division, the die was cast: the 3394 would be retired in May, 1958. As diesels became more numerous on the Great Northern, the O-8's were concentrated east of Williston, North Dakota. Being relatively new, all 25 O-8's remained in service in 1956, continuing to rack up the ton miles, the only class of Great Northern steam still intact. Indeed, their presence delayed complete dieselization until 1957. In the words of GN historian Norman F. Priebe: "The O-8's were great Mikados, the greatest of them all. Those who saw and heard them will agree. None of us will ever forget the bellowing smoke, the blurred rods, the staccato exhaust, and the wild cry of their whistles as they sped freight across the northlands. The O-8's were truly impressive examples of super steampower."

GN 3397

LEFT • In a marvelous portrait of steam at rest, 0-8 #3397 and friend rest in the roundhouse at Minneapolis on May 6, 1956. Built at Hillyard in 1932 and upgraded at Superior in 1946, the 3397 provides ample evidence that steam locomotives are photogenic even in the tight confines of the roundhouse. The photograph is also evidence of why Russ Porter is one of the author's favorite photographers!

RUSS PORTER

CLASS P 4-8-2

CLASS P. MOUNTAIN. The long-limbed, racy locomotives numbered from 2500 to 2527 on the GN were classed as P-2's, and were purchased from Baldwin in 1923 to speed up service on the crack Oriental Limited. The operation was so successful that it led to the inauguration, in 1929, of the first of the luxury Empire Builders. The P-2's then performed distinguished service powering the Fast Mail and the renowned Silk Extras. Note that this 4-8-2 was one of the few Great Northern classes after the turn of the century not to be equipped with the Belpaire firebox.

GN 2510

RIGHT • In a marvelous portrait of a magnificent locomotive, P-2 #2510 with Train #5 waits for the highball at Everett, Washington. It is September 5, 1950 and steam still reigns on the CASCADIAN. Electrics pulled #5 from Wenatchee to Skykomish where the 2510 took over for the remainder of the journey to Seattle. Heavyweight equipment was standard on the CASCADIAN until 1953 when it received modernized coaches. The first car behind the 2510 is an RPO-baggage, the second is a Burlington express car rebuilt from a troop kitchen car, followed by two coaches and a reserved coach-observation-cafe car. Painted in the light olive scheme, the 2510 displays metal green flags. The P-2's had a much cleaner look than most of its contemporaries. In addition to the lack of a Belpaire firebox, the absence of pumps mounted on the smokebox door is a feature unique to the P-2's.

SANFORD GOODRICK

J. J. BUCKLEY

Class P-2, 4-8-2, Series 2500-2527

ABOVE • Standard power for passenger trains on the Great Northern was first the 4-4-0 and then the 4-6-0 and 4-6-2. As passenger trains became longer, heavier (due to steel construction) and express traffic grew (requiring longer stops at stations), those locomotives became inadequate to haul the varnish, especially in mountainous regions. To meet the need of its passenger operations, in 1914 the Great Northern purchased 15 4-8-2 Mountain-type locomotives from Ohio's Lima Locomotive Works. Classed P-1, they shared many characteristics with the O-1 Mikes. Although great pullers, they simply were not fast enough on the GN's varnish and soon were transferred to freight service. In 1928, fourteen years after they were built, the P-1's were rebuilt into Class Q 2-10-2's. However, the solution to the GN's problem of powering passenger trains would not come until 1923 when Baldwin Locomotive Works delivered 28 Class P-2 4-8-2's. These locomotives had 29" x 28" cylinders, 73" drivers and weighed 365,600 pounds. Weight on the drivers was 242,000 pounds with a tractive effort of 54,840 pounds. Well suited for its intended duties, the P-2 became the standard power for the ORIENTAL LIMITED introduced in 1924. The P-2's also were used on the FAST MAIL and their performance on silk trains became legendary. After World War II the P's were relegated to freight service. The class remained intact until the 2501 was retired in 1955.

The 2505 is pictured at an unknown location in Minnesota sometime during the 1950's. In freight service, and recently painted, it sports a red roof. The P-2's were one of the two classes of modern GN steam which did not have Belpaire fireboxes, using instead a radial stay firebox. Apparently this was done to save weight. The P-2 Mountain was one of the better looking steam locomotives and, in the eyes of many, the absence of the Belpaire firebox contributed to the Mountain's sleek lines.

Route Your Freight Great Northern

Between ST. PAUL, MINNEAPOLIS, DULUTH, WINNIPEG, SIOUX CITY, GREAT FALLS, HELENA, BUTTE, BILLINGS, SPOKANE, PORTLAND, SEATTLE, TACOMA, BREMERTON, KLAMATH FALLS, SACRAMENTO, OAKLAND, SAN FRANCISCO, VANCOUVER, B. C., and intermediate points.

ASK THE GREAT NORTHERN FREIGHT REPRESENTATIVE IN YOUR CITY TO HELP YOU SOLVE YOUR SHIPPING PROBLEM OR WRITE

P. H. Burnham Freight Traffic Manager St. Paul, Minn.	B. S. Merritt Western Traffic Manager Seattle, Wash.	C. E. Finley Asst. Freight Traffic Manager St. Paul, Minn.
H. G. Dow Eastern Traffic Manager 233 Broadway New York City, N. Y.	E. C. Warren Asst. Gen. Freight Agent 105 W. Adams St. Chicago, Ill.	C. F. O'Hara Asst. Gen. Freight and Passenger Agent Helena, Mont.	G. F. Hardy, General Freight Agent 757 Monadnock Bldg. San Francisco, Calif.

STEVE BOGEN

GN 2521

ABOVE • GN 2521 is at the King Street Station in Seattle in 1949. Note the centered headlight, another factor contributing to its good looks. The usual GN practice was to mount the headlight above-center and some P-2's, such as the 2510, conform to this practice. The first 18 P-2's delivered were oil burners and the last 10 burned coal but by 1941 these had been converted to burn oil. The P-2's originally were delivered with Style 104 Vanderbilt tenders but soon after their delivery Style 105 tenders, which came from Q-1's, were assigned to the P-2's. At least two P-2's, the 2519 and 2510, received tender's from S-2's. During World War II about half of the P-2's received roller bearings. Earlier, booster units were added to the trailing trucks increasing tractive effort by 12,200 pounds but these were removed by 1929.

DON BALL COLLECTION

CLASS Q 2-10-2

CLASS Q . SANTA FE. Designed for heavy freight service, the 2-10-2 Santa Fe was known as a class Q engine on the Great Northern. No. 2100, a Q-1, was the first of 30 built for GN by Baldwin in 1923. Not shown in the builder's photo is the Franklin booster engine which was later applied by the railway. The conical boiler with Belpaire firebox and the Vanderbilt tender carrying 15,000 gallons of water and 25 tons of coal were intriguing features. Overall design was simple and clean, and is an excellent representation of heavy freight power of the period.

JACK PFEIFER, ED AUSTIN COLLECTION

Class Q-1, 2-10-2, Series 2100-2129

LEFT • Designed for, and utilized in, heavy freight service, the class Q-1 2-10-2's were built by Baldwin Locomotive Works in 1923. The Q-1's had 63" drivers, 31" x 62" cylinders, and weighed 422,340 pounds with 342,490 pounds resting on the drivers. These heavy haulers had a tractive effort of 87,130 pounds. Most of the Q-1's were equipped by the GN with Franklin booster engines which produced an additional 12,200 pounds of tractive effort. Liked by the crews because of the higher rate of pay, the Q's were real rail pounders. Thus, they spent their lives in drag freight service pulling freight at 25-30 mph. The 2122 (BLW #57563), pictured at an unknown location on an unknown date, provides an excellent view of front-end detail on a heavy freight locomotive. The Q's had a very clean design, especially when compared with other GN steam locomotives, but the front-end was pure Great Northern!

Class Q-2, 2-10-2, Series 2175-2189

ABOVE • In 1928, five years after the Q-1's were delivered, the Great Northern rebuilt Class P-1 4-8-2's into 2-10-2's, Class Q-2. The P-1's, designed for passenger service, were too slow for their intended service, thus their short lives. The Q-2's had 29" x 32" cylinders, 63" drivers, and weighed 364,000 pounds, with 290,000 pounds on the drivers. Tractive effort was 76,250 pounds. The Q-2's were lighter than the Q-1's with less tractive effort. To eliminate confusion among dispatchers, both classes of Q's were rated at 76,000 pounds of tractive effort. The 2181, producing a nice plume of smoke at Willmar, Minnesota on November 8, 1953, was built by the Great Falls Shops in 1928 from P-1 1759. For a short period of time in the late 1940's, the 2181 was equipped with 30" x 32" cylinders. The Q's were equipped with Vanderbilt tenders carrying 15,000 gallons of water. In the company of the 2181 is Class O-6 3358.

ROBERT F. COLLINS

GN 2186
ABOVE & BELOW • Ready for a day's work, Q-2 2186 steams at St. Cloud, Minnesota on October 13, 1956. A graduate of the Superior shops, the 2186 was rebuilt from P-1 1753 in 1928. Later in the same day, coupled onto a train, the 2186 is ready to depart St. Cloud.

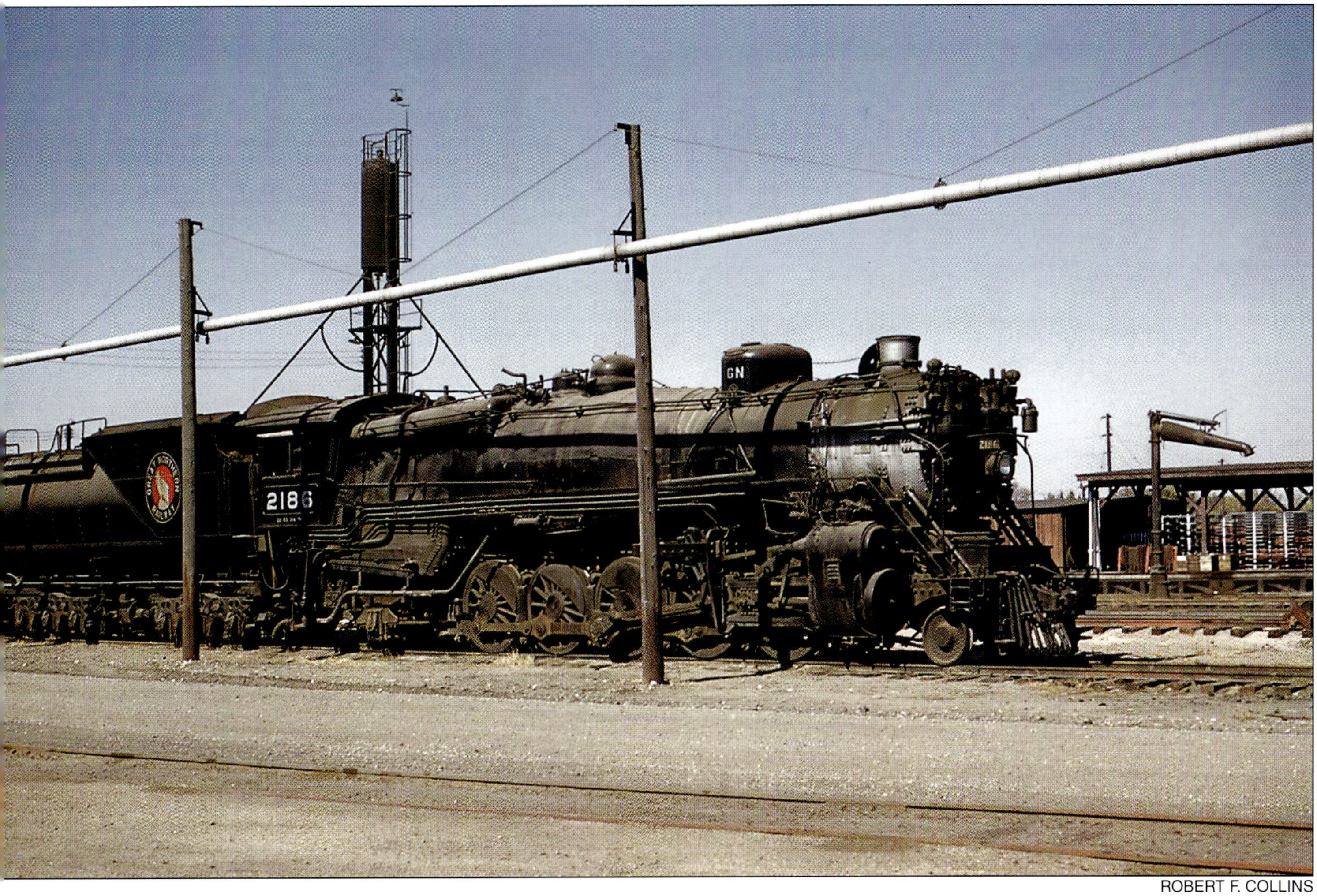

ROBERT F. COLLINS

ROBERT F. COLLINS

GN 2186

ABOVE • On October 4, 1957, one week short of a year later, GN 2186 basks in the sun at Grand Forks. The handsome Santa Fe would be retired by the end of December, 1957.

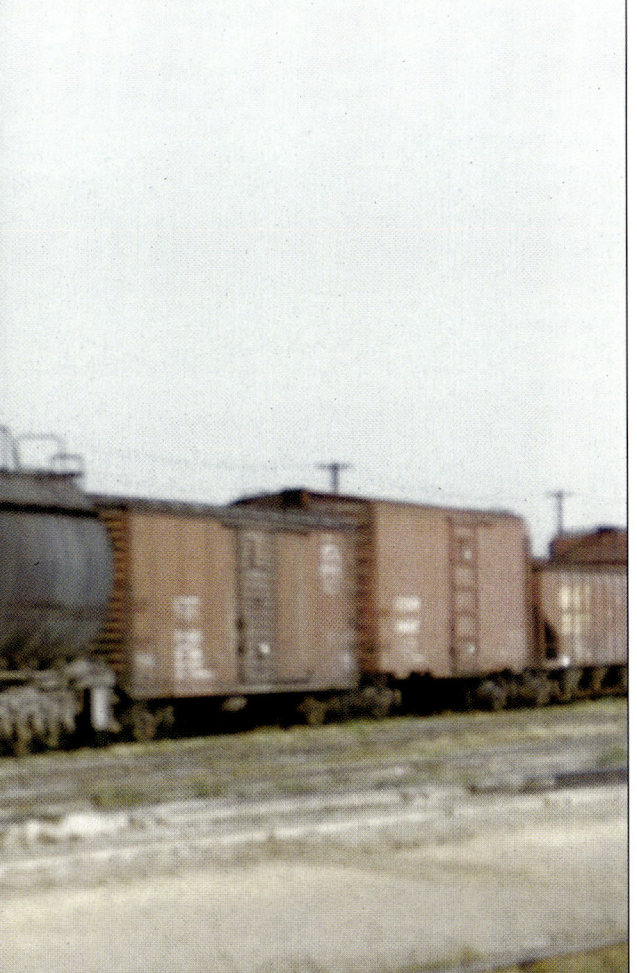

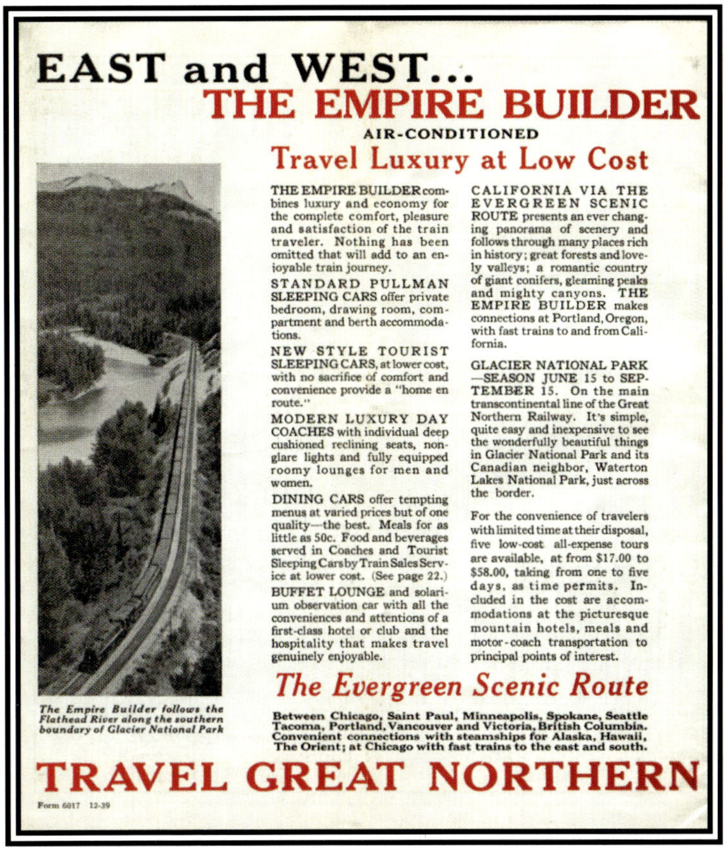

EAST and WEST...

THE EMPIRE BUILDER

AIR-CONDITIONED

Travel Luxury at Low Cost

The Empire Builder follows the Flathead River along the southern boundary of Glacier National Park

THE EMPIRE BUILDER combines luxury and economy for the complete comfort, pleasure and satisfaction of the train traveler. Nothing has been omitted that will add to an enjoyable train journey.

STANDARD PULLMAN SLEEPING CARS offer private bedroom, drawing room, compartment and berth accommodations.

NEW STYLE TOURIST SLEEPING CARS, at lower cost, with no sacrifice of comfort and convenience provide a "home en route."

MODERN LUXURY DAY COACHES with individual deep cushioned reclining seats, non-glare lights and fully equipped roomy lounges for men and women.

DINING CARS offer tempting menus at varied prices but of one quality—the best. Meals for as little as 50c. Food and beverages served in Coaches and Tourist Sleeping Cars by Train Sales Service at lower cost. (See page 22.)

BUFFET LOUNGE and solarium observation car with all the conveniences and attentions of a first-class hotel or club and the hospitality that makes travel genuinely enjoyable.

CALIFORNIA VIA THE EVERGREEN SCENIC ROUTE presents an ever changing panorama of scenery and follows through many places rich in history; great forests and lovely valleys; a romantic country of giant conifers, gleaming peaks and mighty canyons. **THE EMPIRE BUILDER** makes connections at Portland, Oregon, with fast trains to and from California.

GLACIER NATIONAL PARK—SEASON JUNE 15 to SEPTEMBER 15. On the main transcontinental line of the Great Northern Railway. It's simple, quite easy and inexpensive to see the wonderfully beautiful things in Glacier National Park and its Canadian neighbor, Waterton Lakes National Park, just across the border.

For the convenience of travelers with limited time at their disposal, five low-cost all-expense tours are available, at from $17.00 to $58.00, taking from one to five days, as time permits. Included in the cost are accommodations at the picturesque mountain hotels, meals and motor-coach transportation to principal points of interest.

The Evergreen Scenic Route

Between Chicago, Saint Paul, Minneapolis, Spokane, Seattle Tacoma, Portland, Vancouver and Victoria, British Columbia. Convenient connections with steamships for Alaska, Hawaii, The Orient; at Chicago with fast trains to the east and south.

TRAVEL GREAT NORTHERN

Form 6017 12-39

CLASS R 2-8-8-2

CLASS R • SIMPLE ARTICULATED. The mountain-shrinking 2-8-8-0 was the all-time giant of Great Northern's steam fleet—and largest locomotive in the world when Baldwin built the first of its class. Most of the big R's, however, came from the railway's own shops at Hillyard, Washington, and were the first steam locomotives built west of the Mississippi. Heaviest and most powerful of two sub-classes was the R-2, pictured here. Over-all length, with tender, was 119 feet, 11¼ inches; total weight was nearly 530 tons. Twenty-six of these monsters —10 R-1's and 16 R-2's—were constructed in 1927-28.

Class R-2, 2-8-8-2, Series 2044-2059
RIGHT • The first simple articulated 2-8-8-2's on the Great Northern were the Class R-1's, 2030-2033, built by Baldwin in 1925. These were followed by the 2034-2043 built by the GN's Hillyard Shops in 1928. In 1929 and 1930 the Hillyard shops built 16 even larger 2-8-8-2's, #2044-2059, Class R-2. These behomeths were massive and can only be described with superlatives: with tenders they stretched 119'11" over the coupler faces, weighed 621,000 pounds with 436,000 pounds on the drivers. The R-2's had 28" x 32" cylinders and rode on 63" drivers. They produced an astounding 146,000 pounds of tractive effort (some sources state that the R-2's had 153,000 pounds tractive effort), and were the most powerful simple articulates in the world. The R-1's and R-2's were designed for heavy freights on mountain grades. In 1947 and 1948 the R-2's received new boilers built by Alco. The 2044, at Hillyard in May, 1951, provides a nice portrait of the massive R-2's.

GAYLE CHRISTEN

GAYLE CHRISTEN

GN 2051

ABOVE • The 2051, at Hillyard on July 27, 1952, has returned to its birthplace for much needed maintenance. Compare the 2051 with the 2057, opposite page, at Seattle on an unknown date.

RIGHT • During World War II the Great Northern suspended its normal advertising campaign. Instead of soliciting freight traffic and pitching the beauty of Glacier National Park and the Pacific Northwest, the GN emphasized its role in the war effort.

MORNING SUN BOOKS COLLECTION

GN 2057

ABOVE • Adorned in the light olive paint scheme, the 2057 gleams in the sun as it heads for its next assignment. In 1942 all 16 of the R-2's were assigned to the Kalisell Division where they were put to work on the mountain grades. By 1949, equipped with new boilers, the R-2's were split between the Minot and Cascade divisions. The R-2's are a tribute to the GN shops and the Great Northern's policy of building its own locomotives whenever possible, locomotives that would haul maximum ton mileage with minimum train mileage.

LEFT • A Class R 2-8-8-2 rushes crucial war supplies west for shipment to our troops in the Pacific. The Great Northern, like other railroads, was stretched beyond capacity by the demands of war but performed magnificently.

CLASS S 4-8-4

CLASS S • NORTHERN. The powerful and speedy Northern looked every bit the aristocrat that it was during the years of its pre-eminent association with the crack Empire Builder and Oriental Limited trains of the steam era. Baldwin built these 4-8-4's specifically for this service in 1929-30. In later life they powered GN fast freights on eastern districts, and were roller bearing-equipped in 1945. (No. 2578, shown here, was an S-2.) Mounting of the air pump, bell and headlight on the smokebox front was one of the features that gave this engine its massive appearance.

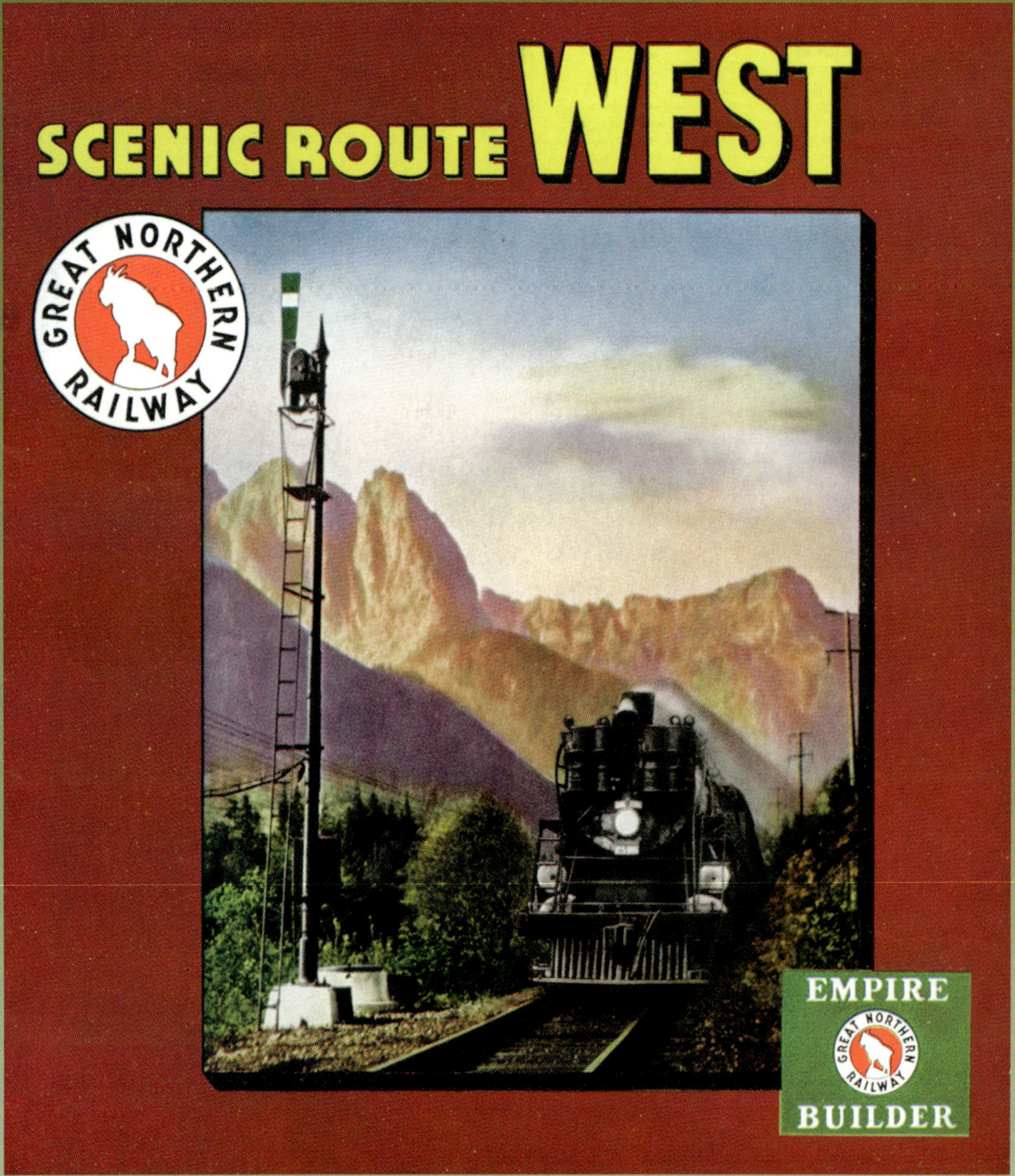

SCENIC ROUTE WEST

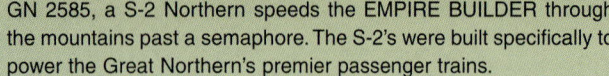

GN 2585, a S-2 Northern speeds the EMPIRE BUILDER through the mountains past a semaphore. The S-2's were built specifically to power the Great Northern's premier passenger trains.

GAYLE CHRISTEN

Class S-1, 4-8-4, Series 2550-2555

ABOVE • Built by Baldwin Locomotive works in April and May, 1929, the 2550-2555 were the first Northerns on the GN. The 4-8-4's cylinders measured 28" x 30". The S-1's rode on 73" drivers, the same as the P-2 Mountains, and with 270,600 pounds resting on the drivers, they had a tractive effort of 68,470 pounds. Having a much longer boiler than the P-2's, the S-1's had about a 20% increase in power over the P-2's. Designed for fast passenger service on the 1% grade west of Havre, Montana, the S-1's had a reputation for being hard on the rails. The 2554 (BLW #60809), at Hillyard on October 9, 1951, provides a good view of an S-1.

GN 2554

RIGHT • Bumped from passenger service by diesels, the S-1's worked at hauling fast freight. Five years later, almost to the day, the 2554 is seen at Grand Forks, North Dakota on October 2, 1956. Whereas the P-2 Mountains were built without the Belpaire firebox, the S-1 reverted back to the usual GN practice of Belpaire fireboxes. Except for the pumps on the front of the smokebox, standard GN practice, the S-1's and S-2's had a smooth, uncluttered look.

DAVID H. HICKCOX COLLECTION

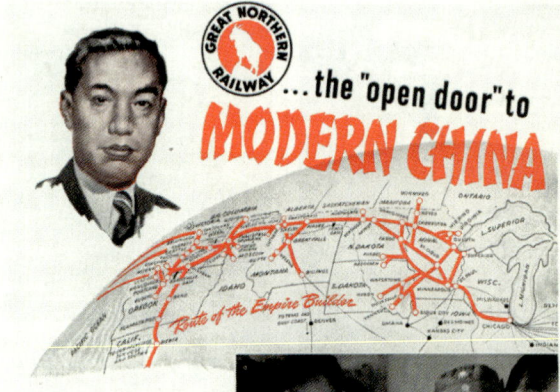

LEFT • Jim Hill always had a strong interest in trade with the Orient. After the cessation of hostilities, and before the takeover of China by the Communist regime, the Great Northern hoped to develop strong trade relations with our World War II allies.

GN 2555

ABOVE • In a magnificent portrait, S-1 2555 (BLW #60810) has just received a new coat of paint at Hillyard. Steaming quietly on a sunny October 9, 1951, the 2555 receives a final touch up before returning to service. By 1951 the S-1 and S-2's were largely removed from passenger service and painted in a more economical black scheme. Some Northerns were kept as protection for passenger trains and that may be the reason the 2555 received the light olive paint scheme. Whatever the reason, we are glad that the Hillyard Shops saw fit to showcase their skills on the 2555.

GAYLE CHRISTEN

J. J. BUCKLEY

Class S-2, 4-8-4, Series 2575-2588

In 1930 the Great Northern received another fourteen 4-8-4's from Baldwin. Differing from the S-1's, the 2575-2588 were classified S-2. With a radial stay firebox, rather than a Belpaire firebox, and with 80" drivers, the tallest on any Northern, the S-2's weighed 420,900 pounds with 247,300 pounds resting on the drivers. Tractive effort was 58,310 pounds, 10,000 pounds less than the S-1. Light for a Northern, the S-2's were fast but tended to be slippery when starting a heavy train. Specifically designed for the ORIENTAL LIMITED and EMPIRE BUILDER, the S-2's were placed in service between Williston, N.D. and Havre, Montana and also between Spokane and Wenatchee, Washington. The S-2's had 29" x 29" cylinders. The covers on the cylinders and steam chest heads were chrome plated. The S-2's had Vanderbilt tenders with all-welded body seams (the only all-welded tenders on the GN) and a capacity of 17,000 gallons of water and 5,800 gallons of oil. Contrary to usual GN practice, the tenders stayed with their locomotives until retirement. Some of the S-2's were temporarily converted to coal burners in the 1930's and all received Timken roller bearings in the 1940's.

ABOVE • S-2 #2584 (BLW #61238) poses somewhere in Minnesota on an unknown date.

BELOW • In a second view, the 2584 is at St. Cloud on October 13, 1956. Removed from passenger service, the high-wheeled Baldwin spent its last years in freight service. Designed for speed, putting an S-2 on a freight train, was, in the words of GN historian Charles Wood, "akin to putting *Man O' War* ahead of a lumber wagon."

ROBERT F. COLLINS

DAVID H. HICKCOX

ABOVE • The 2584 was retired in December, 1957 but on March 21, 1958 was designated "hold for historical purposes." On May 15, 1964 it was put on display at the Havre, Montana depot where it resides today. The author admits to a great deal of fondness for Northerns, and so has included the 2584 on display at Havre on October 30, 1982, all dressed up with nowhere to go.

This undated photograph in Minneapolis symbolizes the changing of the guard. While one steam locomotive is fired up, another sits in a siding, waiting for a call that may never come. Diesels are now more numerous than steam. Definitely, it was the end of an era. But a new era had dawned, one of magnificent color and a wide variety of motive power, the subject of our next book.

MARVIN H. COHEN

BELPAIRE BOILERS & LUMBER

LUTHER GEORGE

LUTHER GEORGE

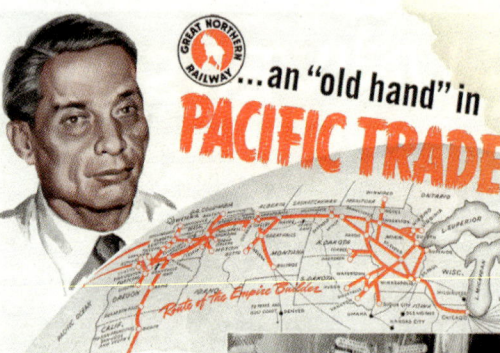

Belpaire Boiler
ABOVE • As most Great Northern fans know, among the major railroads the Belpaire firebox was unique to the Great Northern and Pennsylvania railroads. The GN adopted the Belpaire firebox in 1892 starting with the F-1 Consolidations. Characterized by a flat crown sheet and flat side and roof sheets, which were joined by short radius curves, the Belpaire firebox eliminated the need to strengthen the crown sheet with crown bars. Although more expensive to build, the Belpaire firebox provided increased steaming and water capacity per grate area.

Since the Belpaire firebox was such a unique feature and was a trait shared by two of the country's more noteworthy railroads, we provide two views of the firebox as used on steam locomotives of the Pennsylvania Railroad. First, PRR 9988, a class H-10s 2-8-0 Consolidation, switches at Cleveland Avenue in Columbus, Ohio on October 4, 1957. For purists there is a Great Northern box car in the distance. Class I1s 4524, a 2-10-0 Decapod, was photographed at the same location, also on October 4, 1957. Built to lug-and push-tonnage over mountains, the Pennsy rostered 598 of these powerful workhorses of the Alleghenies.

Somers Lumber Company

ABOVE & BELOW • The forests of western Montana not only provided considerable traffic for the Great Northern but they also provided the ties over which vast amounts of lumber rode to market. A GN subsidiary, Somers Lumber Company, built a tie plant at Somers, Montana, a small town at the north end of Flathead Lake south of Kalispell. The Somers Lumber Company rostered two fireless steam locomotives, the S-1 and S-2. Fire was a major hazard, not only in the sawmill, but especially in the creosoting operation. Thus fireless locomotives were used to lessen the fire hazard. Both the S-1 and S-2 weighed 37,000 pounds. The S-1 was built by H.K. Porter (#7016) in 1926 and the S-2 was built in 1929, also by Porter (#7156). With a steam reservoir in place of a boiler, the two 0-4-0's were charged with steam from a stationary boiler, then went about their business, receiving recharges as necessary. The S-2 moves a cut of creosoted ties in May, 1979. Note the shiny brass bell. Amazingly, the fireless locomotives labored into the 1980's. The development of stringent environmental regulations eventually caused the creosoting operation to close; indeed, decades of creosoting operations led to Somers being declared a "superfund" site by the EPA. Prototypical Great Northern modelers could easily add a creosote and tie plant to a sawmill.

THE END OF STEAM

All good things must come to an end.

The only constant in life is change. Changing technology means changing lives and landscapes. Trite sayings, perhaps, but by the early 1950's it was obvious to all that steam was waning on the Great Northern. World War II had prevented the Great Northern from dieselizing as quickly as management preferred. With restrictions on diesel purchases removed at the end of World War II, the GN began acquiring diesels in large numbers, replacing steam as they were delivered. Dieselization basically proceeded from west to east, placing steam's last stand in Minnesota (For an excellent discussion of the end of steam on the GN see Norman F. Priebe, *Steam's Last Days on the Great Northern*, GNRHS Reference Sheet No. 124). The seasonal nature of the GN's traffic meant a reprieve for steam, especially in 1955 and 1956. Finally, the end was in sight: in August, 1957, steam ran for the last time on the Great Northern.

Our last look at Great Northern steam shows the finality of dieselization: steam stored on deadlines waiting for the call that will never come. The end of steam was truly the end of an era. The changes wrought by the internal combustion engine were numerous and far reaching, changing both the Great Northern's appearance and operations. The extensive infrastructure required to maintain and operate steam locomotives, to include hundreds of structures and thousands of employees, became redundant. Slowly at first, then with a quickening pace, diesels replaced steam. First water treatment plants, then water tanks, coaling towers and eventually roundhouses were destroyed. Even entire yards disappeared as crew districts were lengthened and operating procedures changed. The only constant, it seemed, was change itself. Change, and especially the end of a way of life, can be painful. Yes, it's painful to look at deadlines of steam locomotives but let us not forget the significance of these cold pieces of steel and how the hand of man changed them from inanimate objects of metal to the crowning glory of the Industrial Revolution. Talk to those who operated steam locomotives and they will tell you that each was different, that each was an individual with a personality. Steam made these cold pieces of steel come alive. Before the quickening pace of change removes steam locomotives from Jim Hill's railroad forever, take one last look and remember steam locomotives for what they were, and what they no longer will be. Goodbye, farewell and amen!

RUSS PORTER

GN 818
LEFT • Built by Baldwin (#49243) in 1918, the 818, Class C-1, was photographed at Superior, Wisconsin in October, 1955, three years before it was retired. This angle provides a good view of the Belpaire firebox's angular lines and the detail of the stout switcher's external appliances and piping.

GN 821
BELOW • A comparison of the 821, photographed on October 20, 1957, with the 818 and 821 reveals several differences in small details of the C-1's. The 821 was also built by Baldwin (#49354) in 1918.

W. WOELFER COLLECTION

GN 822
LEFT • At Superior in July, 1958, the 822 still proudly wears a red roof even though rust is becoming prevalent on the drivers and cylinder jackets. Note the difference in headlight placement and the use of number plates vs. number boards on 822 when compared to her sisters. The 822 was also built by Baldwin (#49405) in 1918.

DAVID H. HICKCOX COLLECTION

W. WOELFER COLLECTION

GN 828
ABOVE • The 828 (Baldwin #49658) spent its later years in the Twin Cities area and is shown in St. Paul on October 20, 1957.

GN 832
BELOW • Also at St. Paul on October 20, 1957, GN 832 (Baldwin #51262, built 1919) provides a nice view of its fireman's side. Note that the 832's tender, as well as the other tenders of the C-1's pictured here, are equipped with arch bar trucks. When GN historian Norman F. Priebe photographed the 832 at Minneapolis Junction on August 10, 1957 (see GNRHS Reference Sheet No. 124) he noted that this was the latest photograph of a working steam engine in his collection. Thus, the 832's fire has not been out for long.

W. WOELFER COLLECTION

DAVID H. HICKCOX COLLECTION

GN 3115
ABOVE • O-1 3115 (Baldwin #48775, 1918) is pictured at Superior on an unknown date. While it appears serviceable, the elements have been taking their toll.

GN 2001
BELOW • In 1953 the Class N-3 2-8-8-0's were running between Minot, North Dakota and Breckenridge, Minnesota on the Surrey Cutoff although some had been laid up before that. By 1955 they were in the deadlines. The last years were tough on steam locomotives with limited maintenance, infrequent washings, and bad water. The 2001, which was rebuilt from an N-2 of the same number (BLW X6808-11) at Hillyard in 1941, is at Superior on August 23, 1955. Although its tender appears to be in good shape, the base of the 2001's firebox and its smokebox have accumulated a heavy coat of rust.

LOU SCHMITZ

GN 2006
LEFT • In October, 1955 when visiting the Duluth area, Russ Porter noted that there were 3 tracks of dead steamers at Superior. With dieselization occurring from west to east, by 1954 solid trains of steam locomotives were hauled eastward with Superior the final resting place for many GN steamers. Although high volumes of traffic in the summers of 1955 and 1956 kept steam alive in an increasingly shrinking area in North Dakota and Minnesota, scenes such as this became the rule and live steam the exception.

RUSS PORTER

GAYLE CHRISTEN

GN 2008
ABOVE • GN 2008, at Hillyard in August, 1953, has been pulled from service, its cab windows boarded up, and its connecting rods removed and placed on the running board. The massive N-3 was built in Hillyard in 1941 from N-2 2008 (BLW X6808-15). A bit of green on the cylinders reminds us of the 2008's better days.

GN 2012
LEFT • Parked at the Superior roundhouse in March, 1963, and looking quite forlorn with a covering of snow, the 2012 has the further indignity of having GP-9m 914 and an SD-9 parked next to it, adding insult to injury. The 2012 ended its life where it began: it was built in Superior in 1926 from N-2 2012 (BLW #38228). Although the fires were put out in 1957, GN steam locomotives remained on the property until the early 1960's, first held in reserve at the request of the federal government and later waiting for the price of scrap steel, which had been depressed, to rise.

RUSS PORTER

GN 2015
Impressive even in these less than favorable conditions, GN 2015 slumbers at Superior in early October, 1955. Built at Superior in 1940 from N-2 2015 (BLW #X5880-8), this may be the last photograph taken of the 2015 as it was scrapped within a few days of when Russ Porter snapped this picture.

RUSS PORTER

GN 2019
ABOVE • A resident of the Hillyard deadline, GN 2019 was towed dead to Hillyard as evidenced by the removal of the connecting rods. At Hillyard in August, 1953, the 2019 was built at Superior in 1940 from N-2 2019 (BLW #X5880-6).

GN 3224
BELOW • Photographed in the St. Paul deadline on October 20, 1957, GN 3224 was one of the locomotives that remained in the deadline until 1962, waiting for the price of scrap steel to rise. We saw the 3224 in better days on page 28.

W. WOELFER COLLECTION

GN 3381
BELOW • Even with its cap stacked and nowhere to go, a Great Northern O-8 looks good. At St. Paul on October 20, 1957, the 3381 is seen in better times on page 39. Nine of the O-8's worked their last days on the Mesabi Division in ore steaming service.

W. WOELFER COLLECTION

GN 2552
With its connecting rod sitting on the running board, GN 2552 basks in the sun at Superior in April, 1958. Even the back of a connecting rod and the ungainly Belpaire firebox can't subtract from the aesthetic qualities possessed by the S-1's. The 2552 was built by Baldwin (#60807) in 1929.

RUSS PORTER

GN 2577
S-2 2577 is at St. Cloud on October 13, 1956. Built by Baldwin (#6213) in 1930, the 2577 was not officially retired until 1957.

ROBERT F. COLLINS

MARTIN EVOY III

GN 2523
ABOVE & BELOW • Something strange is happening here! What is a P-2 Mountain doing at the Willmar, Minnesota engine terminal on October 2, 1964? Answer: The Great Northern donated the 2523, built by Baldwin (#57343) in 1923, to the city of Willmar on October 7, 1964. Martin Evoy III, who happened to be passing through Willmar, knew a good picture when he saw it! Today the 2523 is on display at the Kandiyohi County Historical Society in Willmar, just a few yards from former Great Northern rails.

MARTIN EVOY III

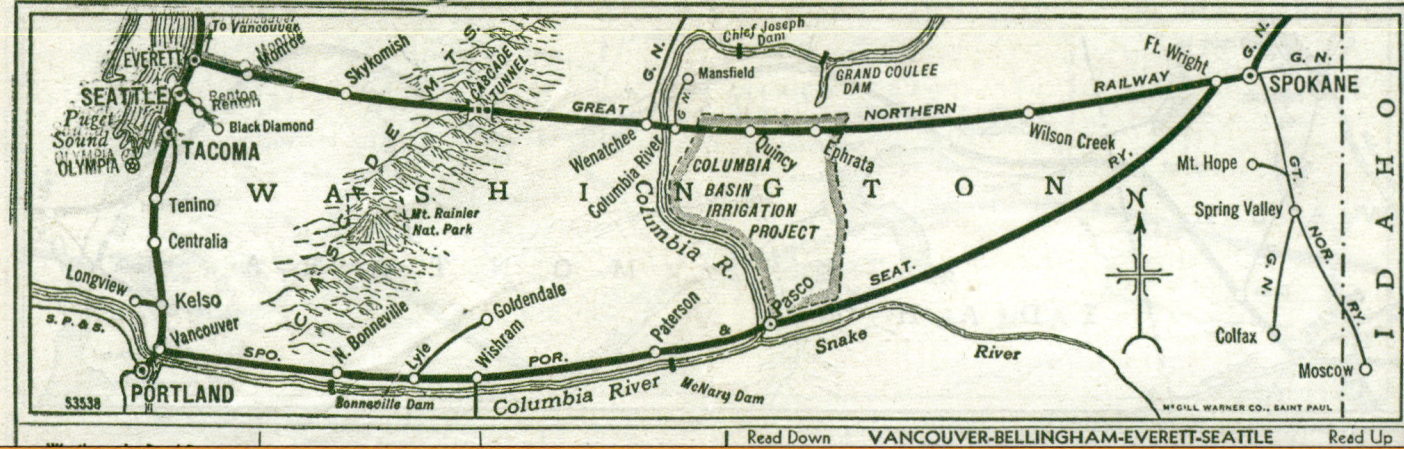

GREAT NORTHERN
ELECTRIC OPERATIONS

Mainline electric operations hold a special fascination. Perhaps it is because of their uniqueness, density of traffic or the difficult, and often remote, territory in which many electrics operated. As a young boy I was convinced that the red and silver Santa Fe F units were the epitome of railroading and that the Pennsylvania Railroad was indeed the "Standard Railroad of the World" (I have since seen the errors of my ways!). But I knew about Great Northern's electric operations. In fact, I knew quite a bit even though Stevens Pass was thousands of miles away. There was something captivating about multiple unit lashups under wire hauling trains up the grade into the Cascade Range and through the famed Cascade Tunnel. I devoured every photograph and word printed about the Great Northern's electric operations that I could find. Mountain railroading, tunnels, snow and avalanches, electric locomotives, even Wenatchee apples. This was a world I could only read and dream about but what marvelous dreams they were! Dreams full of the drama and romance that only railroads could provide to a young train-crazy boy growing up in the 1950's. This was the stuff that legends are made out of.

Legends, yes. But to the Great Northern the Cascade Range was a physical piece of geology that was placed in the way of Jim Hill's route to the Pacific. The mountains were a barrier, all that remained between the Great Northern and Puget Sound. Much has been written about how the Great Northern "Conquered the Cascades." Conquer they didn't. The Great Northern attacked the Cascades in a manner similar to the Marines attacking Guadalcanal. The enemy was formidable and entrenched and it would be much longer than anyone thought before victory was in reach. If the Cascades were conquered then the ensuing peace was quite uneasy. A route with 4 percent grades and numerous switchbacks across Stevens Pass could only be a temporary way of crossing the Cascades. If the topography of the Cascades was challenging, then the long winters with massive snowfall and frequent avalanches were even worse. The Great Northern was at the mercy of the elements each time a train headed up the pass. And winter is not kind to those unprepared for the challenge.

The Great Northern was quick to realize that a tunnel through the Cascades would be necessary. In 1900 the GN completed the first Cascade Tunnel, a 2.63 mile bore that eliminated some, but certainly not all, of the problems of operating across Stevens Pass. The first Cascade Tunnel had a 1.7 percent ruling grade for eastbound trains. Smoke and gas from steam locomotives working upgrade posed serious problems for both crews and passengers. Gas masks were standard equipment in the locomotive cabs but there was no protection for passengers. A stalled passenger train could result in a huge death toll. In 1909 the tunnel was electrified. Boxcab electrics with trolley poles pulled trains and their steam locomotives about three miles, from Wellington on the west end and Cascade Tunnel Station at the east portal. Yet problems remained. Grades and curvature were still excessive and snow and avalanches continued to pose serious problems. Avalanching was exacerbated by fires, no doubt caused by the railroad, and lumber operations which removed large portions of the protective forest. On March 1, 1909, two trains were swept from the tracks at Wellington by a massive avalanche, one of the worst avalanche disasters in the U.S. Almost twelve miles of snowsheds and tunnels were built by the GN to protect the track and trains. These were expensive to maintain and created additional smoke problems. Changing electric locomotives in and out for a three mile run was grossly inefficient. The Great Northern's management realized that a longer tunnel at a lower elevation was needed with a much longer electrified district. Engineering studies were completed as early as 1912 but cost (early plans were for a 14-17 mile tunnel) and World War I delayed construction of the longer bore.

By the early 1920's GN management, under the capable direction of Ralph Budd, was ready to tackle the project of a longer tunnel. Improvements in electric locomotives meant that a shorter tunnel at a higher elevation would be feasible. The Great Northern's plan for finally conquering the Cascades had three parts: First was a single track 7.79 mile tunnel extending from Scenic on the west side of the Cascades to Berne on the east side. This tunnel would remove the GN's tracks from the most dangerous avalanche area, cut curvature, reduce the distance and reduce the elevation of the summit crossing. The second part of Budd's plan was to relocate the line to reduce curvature and grades, eliminating the need for snowsheds and making operation more efficient and less costly. The third part of the plan would extend electrification from Wenatchee, on the west bank of the Columbia River to Skykomish, 72 miles to the west. A modern single-phase power system with a small fleet of new, more powerful electric locomotives would eliminate the problem of smoke, increase speed, allow for heavier trains, increase the flexibility of operations and generally provide much more efficient and less costly operations. Behind the brilliance of the Great Northern's three pronged plan was the ghost of Jim Hill: maximize ton miles while minimizing train miles.

Construction on what was to become the longest railroad tunnel in the western hemisphere began in December, 1925. Using new and more efficient construction methods, work progressed rapidly despite the remote location and difficult working conditions. The tunnel was completed on December 24, 1928, requiring far less time to complete than similar projects. The new Cascade Tunnel was officially dedicated on January 12, 1929. Ralph Budd fittingly stated: "The completed tunnel symbol-

izes the main idea behind the railroad career of James J. Hill; namely, the importance of economy and efficiency in railway operation." While the tunnel was drilled a new yard and service facility was constructed at Wenatchee, the line relocations were built and the infrastructure to support electric operations was put in place. The Great Northern's route through the Cascades was shortened 8.9 miles, 7 miles of snowsheds were eliminated along with 3,674 degrees of curvature, and the elevation of the summit was reduced 502 feet.

Electric operations through the Cascades quickly became routine. With a lower summit elevation, reduction of excessive grades and curvature, elimination of snowsheds, and reduction of the avalanche threat, operations produced the promised efficiencies. Conquering the Cascades was not without cost: the tunnel, line relocation and electrification cost the Great Northern $25.6 million. And 1929 was not the year to begin recovering costs by increasing traffic. However, the ensuing years would soon provide complete justification for the Cascade Tunnel project. Indeed, without the new tunnel and electrified district, the Great Northern would have experienced major problems during World War II when extraordinary demands were placed on the railroad.

The Great Northern's electric operations are presented geographically beginning in Wenatchee. We especially benefit from the photography of Sanford Goodrick, W.C. Janssen and Henry Stange, electric traction aficionados who often travelled together in pursuit of their hobby. In the 1950's before jet transport, interstate highways, and rental car agencies made railfanning quick and easy, for most photographing the Great Northern's electric operations required a major, and expensive, logistical effort. As the throb of diesel locomotives crept closer to Stevens Pass and the Cascade Tunnel, more fans made the effort to photograph electric operations. We have tried to detail the significance of both the electric locomotives and the territory they traversed, beginning in Wenatchee and ending in Skykomish.

ABOVE • Three-phase boxcab electrics exit the west portal of the original Cascade Tunnel. The boxcabs, which were never given a class, were purchased in 1909 to push/pull trains through the original Cascade Tunnel which opened in 1900. With a length of 2.63 miles and an 1.7 percent eastbound grade, the tunnel replaced nine miles of track which featured switchbacks and extremely heavy snowfall. The tunnel, however, was a potential death-trap as long as steam locomotives pulled trains up the grade. Indeed, a train with over 100 passengers narrowly escaped asphyxiation in 1903. Electric operations through the tunnel began in 1909 with four three-phase boxcabs built by Alco and GE. The boxcabs featured pairs of trolley poles (the rails were the third conductor) both fore and aft. Each locomotive generated 1500 horsepower. Using electricity generated by a hydroelectric station on the Wenatchee River near Leavenworth, each boxcab produced a maximum tractive effort of almost 80,000 pounds and could accelerate an 885-ton train on the 2.2 percent grade ruling grade. Only the tunnel, its approaches and the yards at Tye and Wellington near each portal were electrified. This colorized postcard, which was mailed in August, 1910, only a little more than a year after the start of electric operations, shows one of the switchbacks behind the portal and the denuded condition of the mountain slopes which greatly enhanced avalanche problems.

ELECTRIC LOCOMOTIVES

Class ——
5000-5003; built in 1909 by Alco/GE. Operated in first Cascade Tunnel only.
Class Z-1
5000-5001; 5002A-B; 5007A-B; built in 1928 by BLW/Westinghouse; renumbered several times; last renumbering: 5000A-B; 5008A-B; 5002A-B
Class Y-1
5010-5017; built 1927-1930 by Alco/GE; 5011 wrecked in 1945, rebuilt with FT cabs, classified Y-1a.
Class W-1
5018-5019; built by GE in 1947

Source: *The Great Northern Railway Company: All-Time Locomotive Roster, 1861-1970*, Railroad History, Vol. 143 (Autumn, 1980), reprinted by the Great Northern Historical Society.

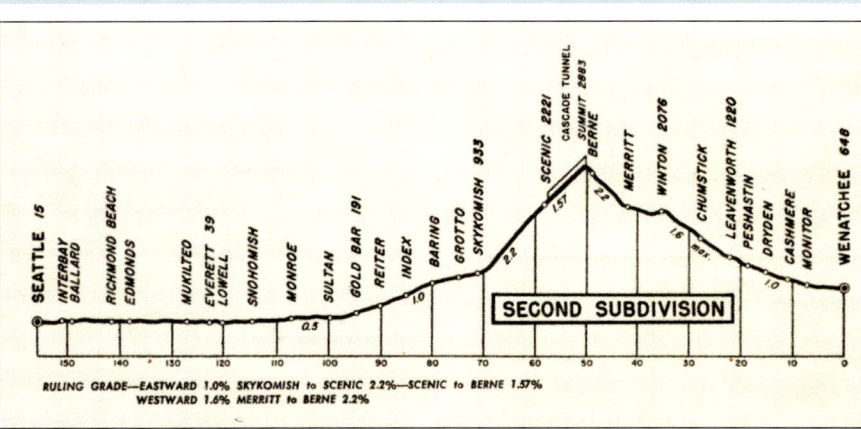

Z-1 5000B

RIGHT • This view of the 5000B, on June 13, 1956, reveals some of the details characteristic of a Z-1. Note the cable receptacles above the 5000B's headlight, roof mounted air reservoirs, a very small pilot and the bell mounted on the side above the trucks and below the cab. With pantographs raised, the 5000 A and B are ready for business. Usually operating in pairs, the Z-1's had long live lives on the Great Northern, remaining on the roster from the time they were delivered until the end of electric operations in 1956.

W. C. JANSSEN

Z-1 5006A

BELOW • The change in division points from Leavenworth to Wenatchee required the construction of a new yard and locomotive facilities. A site on the west bank of the Columbia River south of Wenatchee was selected and construction commenced in 1922, well in advance of the completion of the Cascade Tunnel. Appleyard, as it was named, included icing facilities for refrigerator cars, a roundhouse and steam locomotive servicing facilities, and a four track maintenance shop for electric locomotives. Class Z-1 5006A rests in front of the electric shop on June 10, 1952 with its pantographs down. Built by Baldwin-Westinghouse (#59381) in January, 1927, the 5006A weighed 357,700 pounds with 274,800 pounds on the drivers. Starting tractive effort was 68,700 pounds with a continuous rating of 44,250 pounds. Maximum speed was 38 mph with a continuous rated speed of 14 mph. When coupled together, multiple unit sets of Z-1's could equal or outperform even the most powerful steam locomotive.

EUGENE VAN DUSEN

ABOVE • June 13, 1956, four years later, almost to the day, a three motor set headed by Z-1 5000B and a four motor set headed by 5006A are at Wenatchee. Note the cable receptacles above the 5000B's headlight, roof mounted air reservoirs, a very small pilot, and the bell located under the cab.

SANFORD GOODRICK

BELOW • A broader view of Appleyard's electric facility on the same date provides a good view of the maintenance facility and Class Y-1 #5013. Unlike the Y-1's, which were painted orange and green, the Z-1 motors remained in their original Pullman Green paint.

W. C. JANSSEN

Y-1 5012

ABOVE • The Great Northern rostered eight Class Y-1 electrics, 5010-5017 which were delivered between 1927 and 1930. GN 5012, at Wenatchee on September 5, 1950, was built by Alco-GE (#67542/10537) in September, 1928. Weighing 527,200 tons and delivering 3,000 horsepower, the Y-1's had a 1-C+C-1 wheel arrangement. This scene is rich in details. Note that not all of the yard was covered by catenary—steam, and later diesels, performed most of the yard work. The stores in the foreground are arranged with military precision and the rip track has a good supply of wheels. Box cars from the Southern, Union Pacific and Missouri Pacific are in the background.

ABOVE • During the early 1940s the Great Northern emphasized its contribution to the war effort in its advertising.

HENRY STANGE

HENRY STANGE

Y-1 5016

ABOVE & BELOW • Class Y-1 5016, with both pantographs raised, moves down the track to couple onto a passenger train in Wenatchee on September 5, 1950. The above view provides good detail of the catenary. Note the lights on the depot platform. A large number of reefers are in the background, testimony to Wenatchee's importance as the center of a large fruit growing region. The diesel engine on the Minneapolis & St. Louis flat car is an interesting load. As the 5016 (bottom) gets closer, one can begin to see the details which distinguish a Y-1 from a Z-1. Note the double door box car with its doors open. The 5016 was built in 1930 (ALCO-GE 68274/11151).

SANFORD GOODRICK

Y-1 5016

ABOVE • As the Y-1 slows to couple onto its train, again on September 5, 1950, note the older Great Northern herald with the goat facing forward. This herald was replaced in 1936 by the sideward facing goat. At the time they were built, the Y-1's were the largest single-unit motor-generators in existence and were almost 1½ times heavier and more powerful than a Z-1. Originally the headlight on Y-1's was located on the roof but later was moved to just above the MU cable receptacles. In their place on top of the cab was a device to connect the 11,000 volt A.C. between locomotives for multiple unit operation. The colorful #198 behind the 5016 is an Alco RS-3, built in May, 1950 and later renumbered to 226.

BELOW • The 5016 slows to couple onto its train. It was standard procedure on the Great Northern to have both pantographs up when there was a single locomotive on the train. Note that the air reservoirs are mounted sideways whereas on the Z-1's they were lengthwise. Behind the 5016 is NW2 #135, built in 1942 and one of the earlier diesels the GN purchased. These four scenes of the 5016 were everyday railroading on the Great Northern in 1950, but today represent railroading that most of us can only experience through the efforts of those few who took the time and effort to record the Great Northern's electric operations.

EUGENE VAN DUSEN

W. C. JANSSEN

Y-1 5013

ABOVE • Class Y-1 5013 rests in the company of several other electric locomotives at Appleyard in Wenatchee on June 13, 1956. The Y-1's were almost 74' long and had a maximum tractive effort of 120,600 pounds. The electricity from the catenary was stepped down to 2,300 volts which was then delivered to a synchronous motor which drew two 750 volt D.C. generators operating in series. A GE 290-A traction motor was geared to six pairs of 55" wheels.

RIGHT • The federally owned dams in the Columbia and Missouri river basins generated huge amounts of electricity at low cost. After World War II, the Great Northern hoped to capitalize on this reserve to stimulate industrial development and, subsequently, traffic.

FOLLOWING PAGE; ABOVE & BELOW • Dieselization eventually caused the termination of electric operations on the Great Northern. With the arrival of large numbers of FT's, the end was near. Even though a lashup of Z-1's or Y-1's weighed more and had more horsepower and tractive effort, the FT's were more economical to operate in that they could run across the entire length of the Great Northern without change, were faster and provided a smoother ride. Once Cascade Tunnel was equipped with smoke clearing fans in 1956, the electric motors, regardless of their efficiency, became redundant. In the top photo, an A-B-B-A set of FT's has an eastbound freight in tow on July 16, 1956 at the US 2 overpass on the west edge of Wenatchee. A four unit set of Y-1 helpers can barely be seen just above the bridge in the background. In the lower photo, the helpers, with 5012 in front, approach the photographer. While helpers are mostly thought of in terms of assisting trains upgrade, hence their name, they were also quite useful on downgrade trains. Moving a heavy train down a 2.2% grade with numerous curves was an exercise fraught with hazards. The GN electrics were able to hold back 50% more weight than they were able to pull upgrade. Thus helpers were used both upgrade and downgrade. Note the nature of the vegetation on the hills, a sharp contrast to the rainforest along the west flank of the Cascades. The Cascade Range, extending perpendicular to the flow of moist maritime air blowing east from the Pacific Ocean, creates a barrier over which this air must flow. The result is very dry conditions east of the Cascades.

EUGENE VAN DUSEN

EUGENE VAN DUSEN

ABOVE & RIGHT • Two Y-1's, 5015 and 5013, pull a westbound freight along the Wenatchee River on June 13, 1956. The Y-1 are assisted upgrade by four Z-1's. It was standard procedure to use helpers on all trains over 2,500 tons even if the head locomotives had sufficient power to move the train unassisted. With a ruling grade of 2.2% and numerous curves, a stopped train would be difficult to start without breaking drawbars. The helpers were cut in two-thirds of the way back and so that when starting a considerable strain was taken off the couplers towards the head end of the train. At the maximum grade of 2.2% between Merritt and the height of land inside the Cascade Tunnel, a 5,250 ton train would have the lead locomotives pulling 3,000 tons, or 60 cars, and the helpers pulling 2,250 tons or 45 cars. A four unit set of Z-1's as seen here was both heavier and had more horsepower and tractive effort than a four unit set of FT's. Modelers should take note of the barren hills and rock outcrops as well as the consist of wood, steel, and outside braced 40' boxcars, in a variety of shades of mineral red.

ALL - W. C. JANSSEN

SANFORD GOODRICK

ABOVE • Cashmere, eleven miles west of Wenatchee at 787' above sea level, is a small market town in the Wenatchee Valley. On July 16, 1956 three Y-1's led by 5012 pause in front of the Cashmere depot while in the background is their eastbound freight with one Y-1.

RIGHT • Packed by on-line Cashmere Pioneer Growers (note the steam locomotive), "Empire Builder" apples salutes Jim Hill who played a major role in developing and financing the apple industry in and around Wenatchee.

BELOW • Having coupled onto the eastbound, the four Y-1's led by the 5012 moves past the Cashmere depot. Note the vintage trucks. In the background the lower slopes are dotted with apple orchards while snow is still found high in the Cascades.

EUGENE VAN DUSEN

ABOVE • The Wenatchee River, fed by the melting snowpack of the Cascade Range, was put to work, first generating hydroelectricity for the Great Northern in Tumwater Canyon, and then was used to irrigate fruit orchards on the floodplain and alluvial terraces along the river from Wenatchee west about 35 miles. On June 13, 1956, Y-1's 5015 and 5013 pull the same freight as pictured on pages 82 and 83 up the Wenatchee River Valley, surrounded by apple orchards. The combination of abundant water for irrigation, excellent growing conditions and access to market via the Great Northern led to the Wenatchee Valley to becoming one of the country's premier apple growing districts.

BELOW • Crossing the rapidly flowing Wenatchee River, the 5015 and 5013 continue their westward trip to climb towards Stevens Pass. GN operating rules prohibited loaded placarded tank cars from operating nearer than 6 or 16 cars, depending on the contents, from the engine so the tank car behind the 5015 and 5013 is either empty or has a benign cargo.

SANFORD GOODRICK

HENRY STANGE

SANFORD GOODRICK

PREVIOUS PAGE & ABOVE • On September 5, 1950, Henry Stange and Sandy Goodrick rode #5, the westbound CASCADIAN. At Cashmere it met #6, the eastbound CASCADIAN, an event duly recorded from the #5's observation platform. Pulled by the streamlined Y-1a 5011 and Y-1 5010, the CASCADIAN provided service "through the Cascades by daylight" between Spokane and Seattle. An all stops local, the CASCADIAN provided mail, express and passenger service to the small, and often isolated, towns and villages along its route. In the first picture we get a closeup view of the 5011 and also an excellent view of the right-of-way and catenary. Next, we see both the 5011 and 5010 as they past #5. Lastly, the reserved seat coach-cafe-observation, complete with drumhead, passes. Prior to receiving semi-streamlined equipment in 1953, the standard consist for the CASCADIAN was a RPO-baggage-express car, two or three coaches and a coach-cafe-observation car. Inaugurated in 1929, the CASCADIAN provided a very scenic, but very slow, daylight traverse of the state of Washington.

ABOVE & BELOW, NEXT PAGE, TOP • The 5015 and 5013 are on the point of a westbound freight west of Wenatchee on June 13, 1956. The elevated view provides a good view of the roof detail. The roofs were constructed with three hatches to facilitate removal of electric components for repair. Apple orchards extended along the Wenatchee River for about thirty-five miles west of Wenatchee and appear in many photographs of electric operations along this stretch of track.

W. C. JANSSEN

W. C. JANSSEN

W. C. JANSSEN

LEFT • "Jim Hill" apples salutes the Empire builder who not only brought the Great Northern to Wenatchee, but played an instrumental rose in the development of Wenatchee's apple industry.

W. C. JANSSEN

ABOVE & BELOW • With forested mountain slopes in the background, Z-1's 5004-A&B have stopped their westbound train for a meet with an eastbound. Continuing its trip upgrade, the Z-1's pass the depot in Peshatin. There is still some snow in the mountains in this June 13, 1956 view but down in the valley the orchards are well on their way towards producing another crop of apples which will, of course, be transported to market by the Great Northern in Western Fruit Express reefers.

W. C. JANSSEN

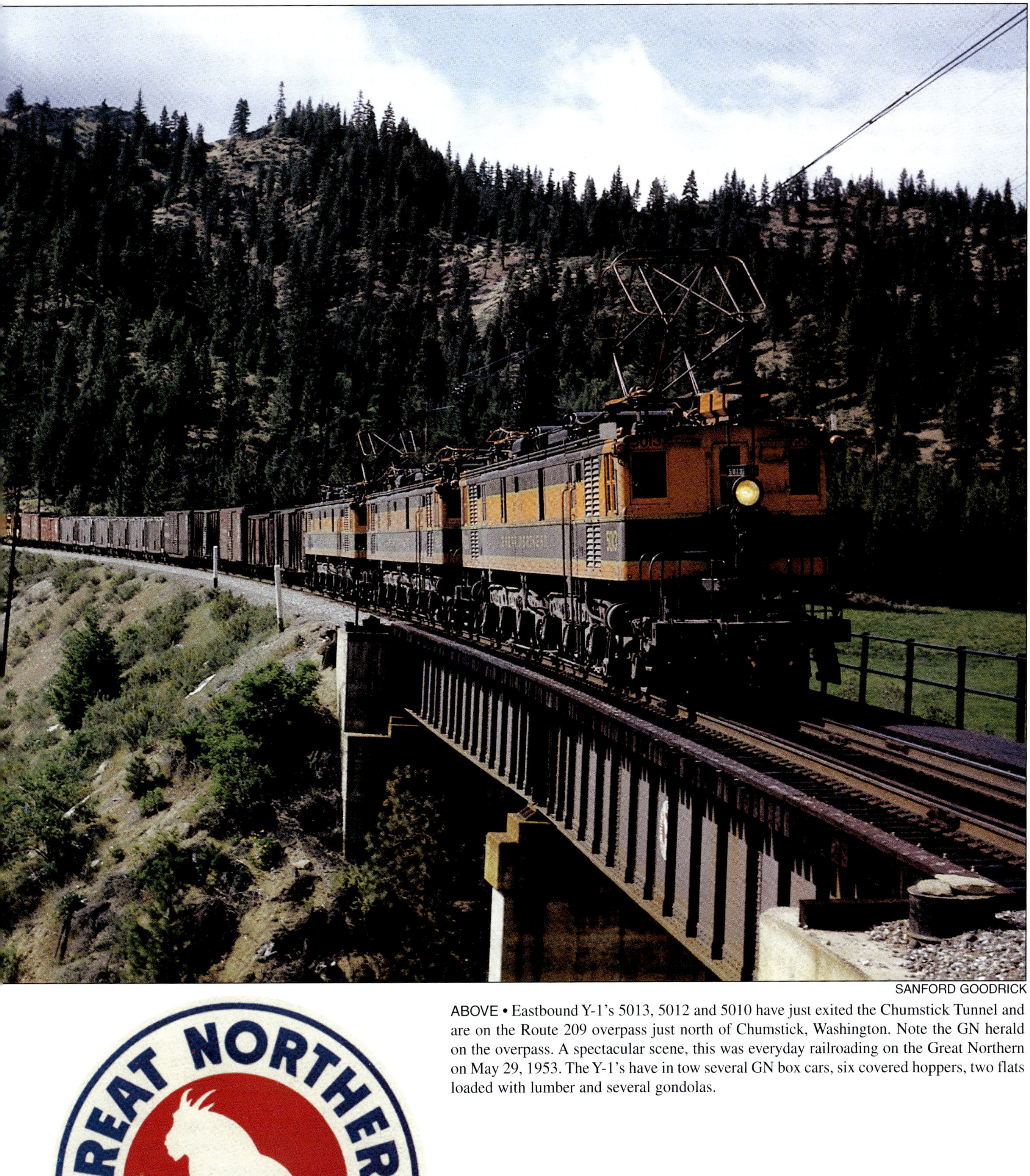

SANFORD GOODRICK

ABOVE • Eastbound Y-1's 5013, 5012 and 5010 have just exited the Chumstick Tunnel and are on the Route 209 overpass just north of Chumstick, Washington. Note the GN herald on the overpass. A spectacular scene, this was everyday railroading on the Great Northern on May 29, 1953. The Y-1's have in tow several GN box cars, six covered hoppers, two flats loaded with lumber and several gondolas.

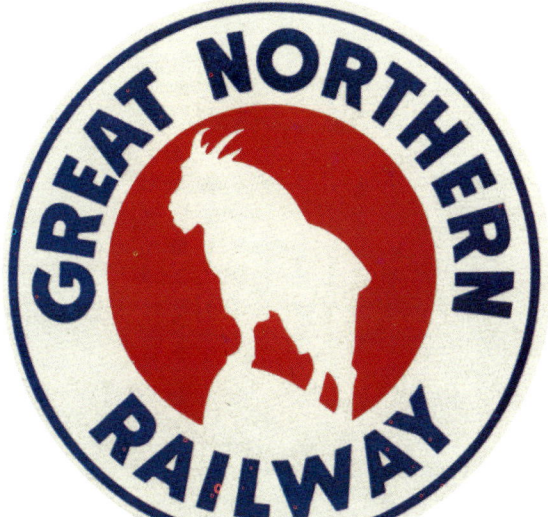

LEFT • GN luggage sticker

SANFORD GOODRICK

ABOVE • Following the eastbound Y-1's Sanford Goodrick photographed them west of Leavenworth. With arrowleaf balsamroot blooming in the foreground, the Y-1's pass through a typical east slope scene.

ABOVE RIGHT • Shortly afterwards, the three Y-1's are again photographed across a field. Fire, probably ignited by GN steam locomotives, and overgrazing have taken their toll on the slopes in the background. Note the outside braced box cars in the consist, especially the GN 50' box car at the picture's edge.

BOTTOM • Lastly, the 5013 and mates were photographed at the overpass west (compass direction north) of Leavenworth.

SANFORD GOODRICK

SANFORD GOODRICK

SANFORD GOODRICK

ABOVE & FOLLOWING PAGE • While photographing the eastbound 5013 on May 29, 1953, Sandy Goodrick encountered a westbound powered by mammoth W-1 5019. Impressive any way you look at it, the 5019 was built by General Electric in 1947. Weighing 735,000 pounds and generating 5,000 horsepower, the 5019 was photographed west of Leavenworth in the company of a heater car. The consist includes a cut of covered hoppers, logs and rough cut lumber in gondolas, heavy equipment on flat cars, two hoppers loaded with coal, and the ubiquitous mineral red box car.

SANFORD GOODRICK

SANFORD GOODRICK

SANFORD GOODRICK

ABOVE • Showing off its immense size (101' long), the 5019 is westbound at Chumstick, also on May 29, 1953. Prior to 1947, the Great Northern relied on boxcab locomotives, first the early three-phase electric motors, then the Z-1's and later the Y-1's. The demands of World War II, which severely taxed the GN's electric operations, and the optimistic outlook for postwar traffic led to the purchase of two 5,000 horsepower electric locomotives. With a streamlined design, the two W-1's had 12 traction motors in a B-D-D-B wheel arrangement (with its 4-8-8-4 wheel arrangement and great length and weight, some have said the W-1's were the "Big Boys" of electric locomotives). From an operations standpoint, one W-1 was the equivalent of two Z-1's although the W-1's had a much larger continuous horsepower rating. The two W-1's were the GN's only modern electric locomotives even though an experimental demonstrator, which later became the Pennsy's class E2b, was tested.

W. C. JANSSEN

ABOVE & BELOW • Y-1's 5015 and 5013 power a westbound upgrade on June 12, 1956 near Chumstick. That is a nice Rock Island PS-1 box car with black ends and a "Route of the Rockets" slogan. As the 5015 passes over Route 209, there's a big wave from the cab.

W. C. JANSSEN

JAMES P. SHUMAN

ABOVE • For the first several miles west of Wenatchee, westbound trains encountered a grade of 1%. From Wenatchee, elevation 648', west to Leavenworth, elevation 1,220', a total of 572' in elevation was gained in twenty two miles, an average of 26 feet per mile. West of Leavenworth, the grade steepened to a maximum of 1.6% between Leavenworth and Winton, elevation 2,076'. A total of 856 feet was gained in this 13.55 mile stretch of track for an average of 63.2 feet to the mile. The grade slacked off a bit from Winton to Merritt but from Merritt to the top of the grade in the Cascade Tunnel, elevation 2,883 feet, the ruling grade was 2.2%. For eastbound trains the ruling grade from Skykomish, elevation 933 feet, and Scenic, elevation 2,221feet, was 2.2%. In this 12.76 mile stretch 1,288 feet were gained, an average of 100.9 feet per mile. From Scenic to the crest of the grade the ruling grade slackened to 1.57%. These grades and the 7.79 mile Cascade Tunnel were, of course, well suited for electric operations, especially when the only alternative was steam. For decades the Cascade Range was the Great Northern's weak point. But electric motors operated in unison, such as the 5003 and two other Y-1's pictured on May 29, 1953, brought the GN's operation through the Cascades more in line with the Empire Builder's philosophy of maximum efficiency and economy.

BELOW • Several Z-1's, led by 5002-B, pull tonnage upgrade at the west end of Berne siding on May 29, 1953. This photograph conveys the sense of no-nonsense railroading that characterized the Great Northern's crossing of the Cascade Range. It's all business here as the Z-1's near the Cascade Tunnel. Note the metal numbers nailed to the pole. The 1699 identifies the station as Berne (consult a Cascade Division employee timetable for a listing of station numbers). The low clouds covering the mountains are quite typical for this time of year.

SANFORD GOODRICK

SANFORD GOODRICK

ABOVE • Even with the construction of Cascade Tunnel and line relocations that reduced curvature and grades, Stevens Pass remained a tough piece of railroading as illustrated by this rock cut east of Cascade Tunnel, pictured on September 5, 1950. Clearances were quite tight, curvature was a constant, and the mountain grades were unforgiving. For the engineer of a train crossing Stevens Pass, reaching the summit was not an invitation to relax as bringing a train down a 2.2% grade was even more demanding than the uphill climb. Mountain railroading and complacency were by necessity mutually exclusive! GN modelers should take note of the rock formations and their weathering, the vegetation and the details of the right-of-way, catenary and pole line.

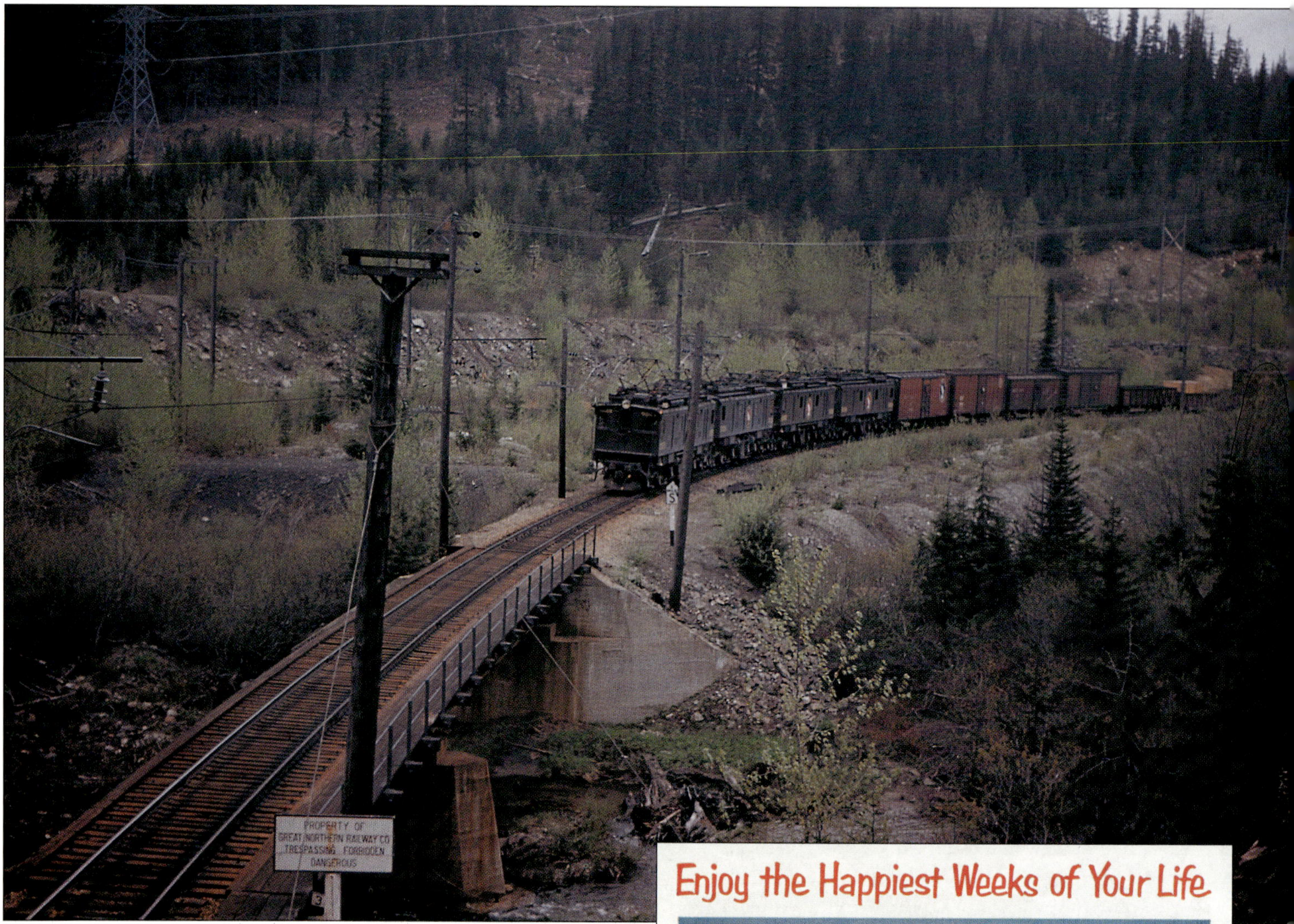
PROPERTY OF
GREAT NORTHERN RAILWAY CO
TRESPASSING FORBIDDEN
DANGEROUS

SANFORD GOODRICK

ABOVE & FOLLOWING PAGE • The four Z-1's approach the east portal of Cascade Tunnel. US 2, utilizing the old GN grade, crosses directly above the east portal, affording an excellent vantage point for photography. The four motor set, a typical lashup in this May 29, 1953 view, crosses the bridge at the tunnel entrance. Cut into the train two-thirds of the way back are two helpers, one of which is the distinctive Y-1a 5011. Soon it will be all downhill to Skykomish where the electric locomotives will be cut out. The regenerative breaking power of the electrics will be most helpful in negotiating the 2.2% grade between Scenic and Skykomish.

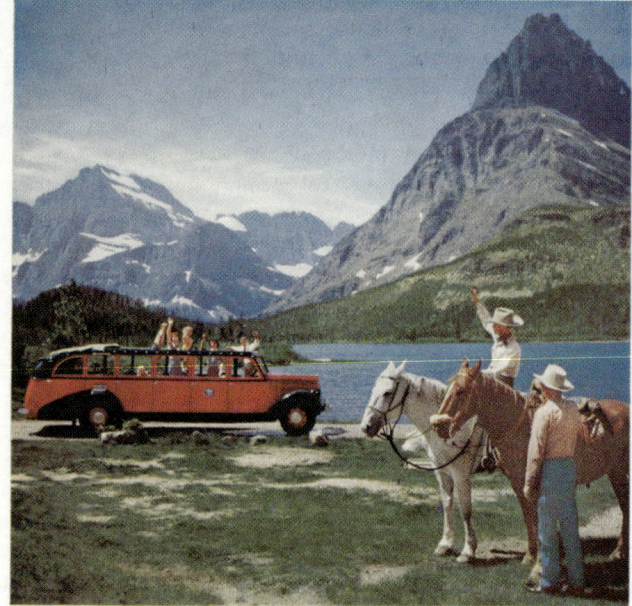

Enjoy the Happiest Weeks of Your Life
Riders of trail and road at Swiftcurrent Lake.
in Glacier National Park
'way out West in the Montana Rockies
For the rest of your life you'll treasure the memories of a vacation spent in the rugged wilderness of Glacier National Park. Never-to-be-forgotten delights: wonderful hotels, marvelous meals, adventure on the mountain trails either on horseback or hiking.
Go Great Northern . . .
Great Northern streamliners take you to the very doors of Glacier Park. So your vacation starts the moment you board the Western Star.
For information or reservations on travel to Glacier Park and other Western vacation areas, write P. G. HOLMES, Passenger Traffic Manager, Dept. N-47, Great Northern Ry., St. Paul 1, Minn., or consult your nearest ticket or travel agent.
GREAT NORTHERN RAILWAY

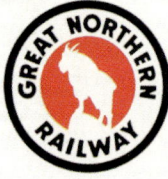

SANFORD GOODRICK

SANFORD GOODRICK

EUGENE VAN DUSEN

ABOVE • Y-1a 5011 and Y-1 5017 negotiate the curve at the east portal of Cascade Tunnel on August 10, 1952. Note that the 5017 has orange pantographs! From the east portal to the west portal the 7.79 mile tunnel drops 634 feet. The Cascade Tunnel reduced the elevation of the summit from 3,383 feet (the original crossing of Stevens Pass had an elevation of 4,068 feet and grades of 4%) to 2,883 feet, while eliminating 1,940 degrees of curvature and almost 40,000 feet in snowsheds as well as several bridges.

THE CASCADIAN
Air-Conditioned
THROUGH THE CASCADES BY DAYLIGHT
Daily between Seattle and Spokane

One of the most beautiful scenic rail trips in America. A daylight ride along Puget Sound, across the Cascade Mountains and through the famous eight-mile electrified Cascade Tunnel.

Air-conditioned cafe-coach (reserved-seats) and modern coaches. Individual chairs at only 50c additional. Food service, table d'hote and a la carte, for as little as 50c. Sandwiches, pie (10c) and hot coffee (5c) served by Train Sales Service. (See list on page 22.) Request your local ticket agent or travel bureau to arrange this trip when buying your ticket.

102

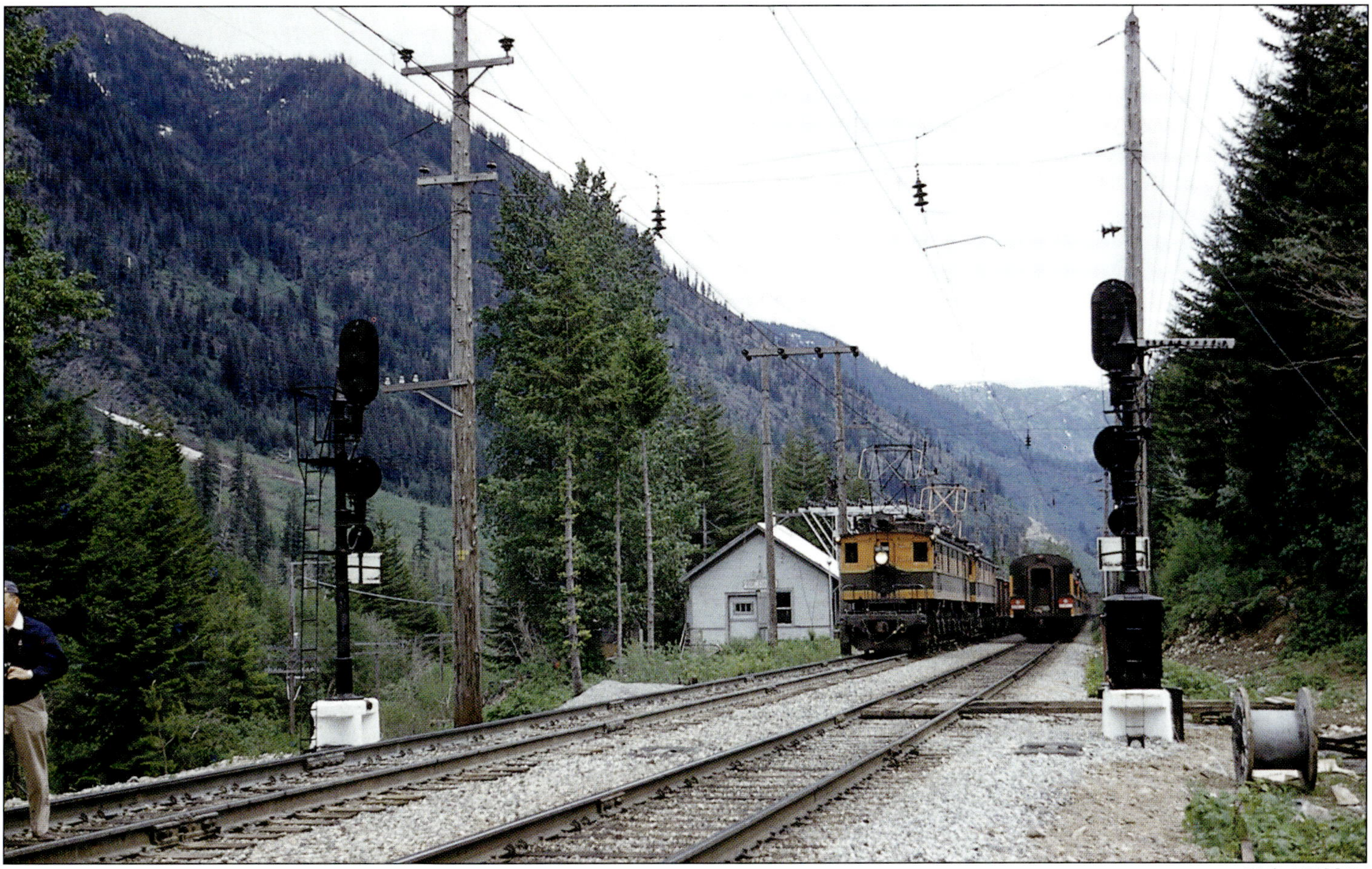

W. C. JANSSEN

ABOVE & BELOW • Train # 6, the eastbound CASCADIAN, rushes past Berne and a westbound freight powered by Y-1's 5015 and 5013 on June 13, 1956. The grade from the beginning of the Chumstick line to the East Portal was 2.2% and an idea of that grade can be seen in the above photograph. Operating conditions required a siding east of the east portal where westbounds would wait their turn to enter the tunnel. With tremendous tractive effort and starting horsepower, the Y-1's had no problem starting a train on the 2.2% grade, especially with helpers cut in two-thirds of the way back, although care had to be taken not to pull drawbars. Once the CASCADIAN clears Berne, the 5015 will pull its train up the final approach to the Cascade Tunnel.

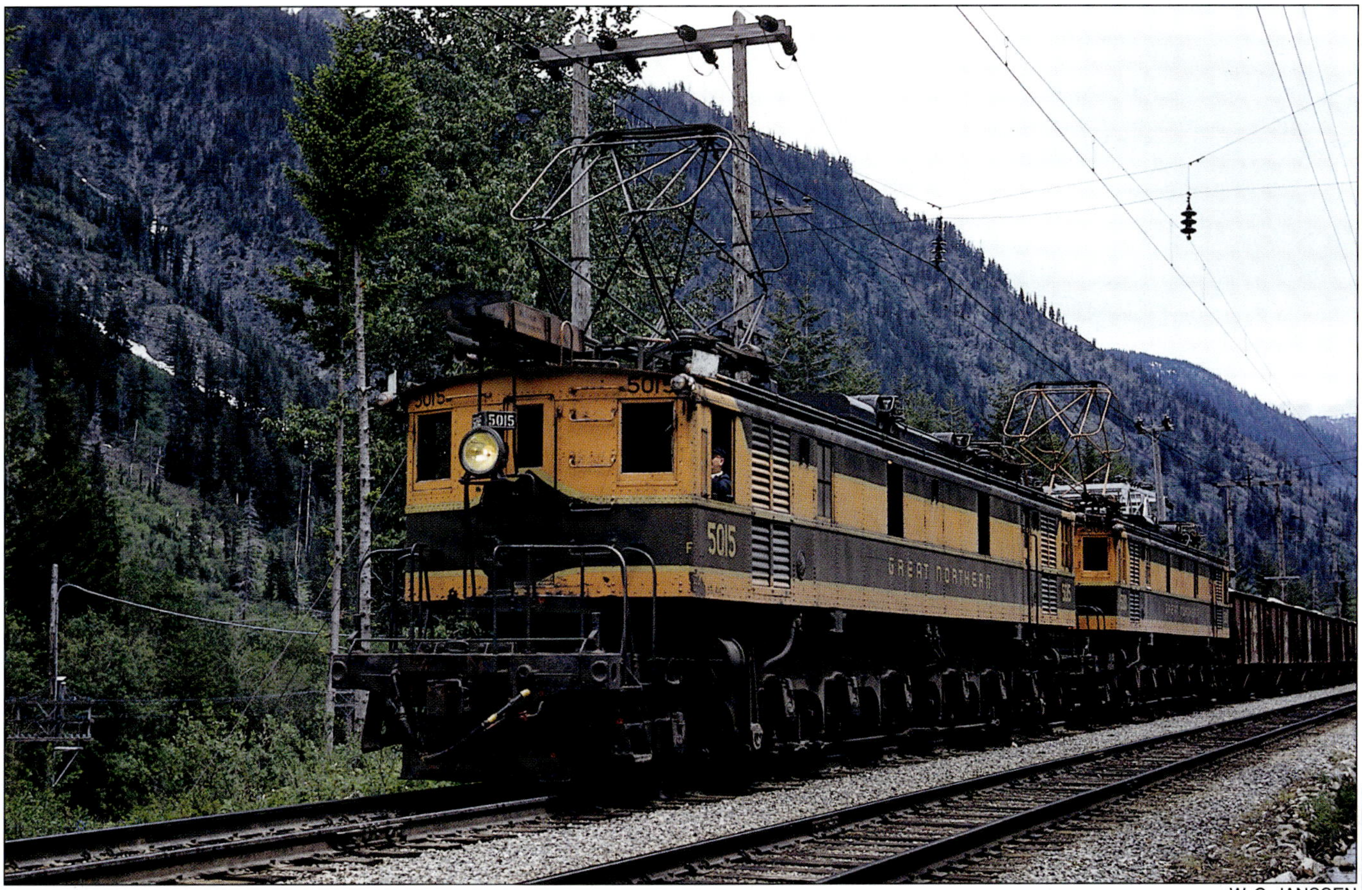

W. C. JANSSEN

W. C. JANSSEN

HENRY STANGE

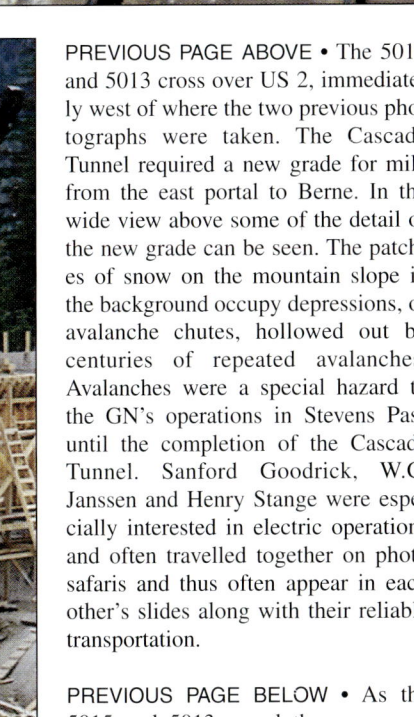
W. C. JANSSEN

PREVIOUS PAGE ABOVE • The 5015 and 5013 cross over US 2, immediately west of where the two previous photographs were taken. The Cascade Tunnel required a new grade for mile from the east portal to Berne. In the wide view above some of the detail of the new grade can be seen. The patches of snow on the mountain slope in the background occupy depressions, or avalanche chutes, hollowed out by centuries of repeated avalanches. Avalanches were a special hazard to the GN's operations in Stevens Pass until the completion of the Cascade Tunnel. Sanford Goodrick, W.C. Janssen and Henry Stange were especially interested in electric operations and often travelled together on photo safaris and thus often appear in each other's slides along with their reliable transportation.

PREVIOUS PAGE BELOW • As the 5015 and 5013 round the curve and prepare to enter the tunnel in this June 13, 1956 view, construction is well under way on the new ventilation system. Consisting of two 6' fans, the increased ventilation will allow diesels to operate through the tunnel, making electric operations redundant.

THE CASCADE TUNNEL

One of America's greatest engineering accomplishments, is 7.79 miles long, absolutely straight from end to end, and on a grade of 1.56 per cent descending from east to west. The construction was authorized Thanksgiving Day, the contract let November 27, 1925. Actual work began immediately. Solid granite was encountered practically throughout. The bore is entirely lined with concrete, is electrified and ventilated.

The official opening took place and the first train the "Empire Builder" passed through on January 12, 1929— 37 months from the time the first shovel of dirt was removed. Completion of the tunnel and the construction of 19.37 miles of new road on the east slope of the Cascade Range through the Chumstick Valley, and electrifying the line from Appleyard, near Wenatchee to Skykomish on the west slope, formed a three-fold improvement, which shortened the distance by 8.88 miles, eliminated many miles of snow sheds and transformed a slow tedious route over the Cascades into a uniform easy grade line affording fast, clean and pleasant travel.

ABOVE • The west portal of the 7.79 mile Cascade Tunnel is at an elevation of 2,247 feet. The tunnel has a grade of 2.57% from the west portal to the height of land at 2,883 feet. The scar on the mountain above the tunnel entrance, now the route of US 2, was part of the GN's original line across Stevens Pass. Formally opened on January 12, 1929, the Cascade Tunnel was at the time the longest tunnel in the Western Hemisphere. An elaborate opening ceremony was held including a nationwide radio broadcast on NBC, with a speech by President Hoover, and a special train with reporters and dignitaries running from east to west, breaking through a cover of paper, officially signifying that the tunnel was open. Once the tunnel was open electric operations between Skykomish and Wenatchee became routine and generally trouble free. The appearance of the west portal has remained unchanged over the years although a dense cover of trees has grown up around it.

W. C. JANSSEN

ABOVE & FOLLOWING PAGE • In a three photo sequence Y-1's 5015 and 5013 bring a westbound freight downgrade out of the west portal of Cascade Tunnel on June 13, 1956. The completion of the tunnel required a relocation of track from just west of Scenic to the west portal. While the tunnel eliminated the worst of the steep grades that plagued Stevens Pass, there were short stretches of 2.2% grade on both the east and west approaches to the Cascade Tunnel. With a cut of ballast cars on the head end, the Y-1's use their regenerative braking on the steep grade. While the west portal is readily accessible today, photography of contemporary operations is more difficult due to the regrowth of a dense forest. In earlier years logging and forest fires, many started by sparks or cinders from GN trains, cleared much of the forest from the mountain slopes adjacent to and above the tracks through Stevens Pass. Deforestation unfortunately triggered a dramatic increase in the number of avalanches and snowslides, greatly hindering operations through the pass. The worst disaster occurred on the night of March 1, 1910 at Wellington when a massive avalanche swept two trains from the tracks killing 101 people. The Cascade Tunnel removed the Great Northern from much of the snow hazard. Note that even on June 13 patches of snow still remain in the vicinity of the west portal.

W. C. JANSSEN

W. C. JANSSEN

ABOVE • In a scene rich in detail, the 5019, its white "flags" flying, runs downgrade past Scenic on July 16, 1956, no doubt using the huge electric's regenerative braking. The 5019 dwarfs the F units behind it. Note the former baggage car with truss rods and a curved roof.

EUGENE VAN DUSEN

HENRY STANGE

ABOVE • Taken from the rear of train #5, the westbound CASCADIAN, on September 5, 1950, we get an excellent view of Scenic. A steam powered maintenance of way train sits in the siding. The train order signal indicates clear and orange track vehicles sit at each end of the depot. The bridge over the tracks carries US 2 which can be seen winding its way up the mountain above the bridge. The development of US 2 into a modern all-weather road across the Cascades caused a dramatic decrease in the number of passengers riding the CASCADIANS.

ABOVE • From Scenic downgrade to Skykomish, the western terminus of electric operations, is a distance of 12.76 miles. The ruling grade on this stretch of track is 2.2%. The 5015 and 5013, which we first saw at Berne, is rolling downgrade between the west portal and Skykomish. With a long and heavy train, the regenerative breaking power of the two Y-1's keeps the train under control. The maximum speed limit for freights between Merritt and Skykomish was 20 mph (30 mph for passenger trains) and this limit was rigorously enforced.

BELOW • Skykomish was the western terminus for electric operations and had a small yard with facilities to service electrics, steam and diesels. On June 13, 1956, four Z-1's move away from the sand tower, ready to help an eastbound over Stevens Pass. There is a nice assortment of camp cars in the yard.

W. C. JANSSEN

W. C. JANSSEN

ABOVE • Z-1's 5002B & A sit in Skykomish on June 10, 1952. Except for renumbering and an updated herald, the external appearance of the Z-1's changed little since their delivery in 1926, 1927 and 1928.

BELOW • Coupled to the 5002B and 5006A, the 5002A basks in the sun at Skykomish on August 1, 1955.

EUGENE VAN DUSEN

MONTY POWELL, LOU SCHMITZ COLLECTION

MONTY POWELL, W. WOELFER COLLECTION

ABOVE • With their pans up the 5000B and 5000A await a call to action at Skykomish on August 5, 1955.

RIGHT • The 5000A is at Skykomish on July 30, 1955. The close in view, looking up at the 5000A, provides a good view of the Y-1's detail.

ROBERT MORRISON COLLECTION

DON BALL COLLECTION

LEFT • In a scene rich in detail, several electric motors wait in Skykomish for the call to action on June 24, 1955. The low clouds hint of the Cascade Range's notoriously bad weather. Four Z-1's, with the 5006A in the lead, share a track with a rotary snowplow and its tender. Y-1a 5011 and one of the W-1's also rest at the engine terminal while a steam locomotive works in the distance. The electrics were maintained in Wenatchee; Skykomish had a small building where the electrics could be pulled out of the elements for minor work. Servicing facilities for steam locomotives are in the background as is the imposing electricity generating plant.

BELOW • Y-1 5010, with green flags, moves along the track at Skykomish on September 5, 1950. The 5010, completed in August, 1927, was the first Y-1 built, and was followed by the 5011 in September. The other Y-1's, were delivered in 1928 (5012-5013) and 1930 (5014-5017). Since all eight (5010-5017) Y-1's were painted into the orange and green scheme in the early 1950's, color photographs of them in their original paint are few in number. Even rarer are color photographs of GN maintenance-of-way equipment in gray. The 5010 passes by several ancient MOW cars, all of which except the 02544 proudly display the GN herald.

SANFORD GOODRICK

ABOVE • Y-1 5014 and two others bask in the sun at Skykomish with their heater cars in 1949. Note the two gray MOW cars in the distance, especially the venerable truss rod car with arched windows. The class Y and class W electrics were not equipped with boilers for heating passenger trains, thus boiler-equipped heater cars were a necessity.

STEVE BOGEN

BELOW • With heater car #7 in tow at Skykomish on June 10, 1952, the 5015 is ready to take the eastbound CASCADIAN to Wenatchee.

EUGENE VAN DUSEN

W. C. JANSSEN

ABOVE • Having completed their westbound journey to Skykomish, the 5015 and 5013 cut off from their train. Waiting on the next track are the F-units which will power the train to Seattle.

BELOW • The 5015 and 5013 stop in front of the depot to wait for an eastbound train. There is still a lot of snow in the mountains on June 13, 1956.

W. C. JANSSEN

MONTY POWELL, LOU SCHMITZ COLLECTION

ABOVE & BELOW • The 5015 and 5016 sit at Skykomish on July 31, 1955 with their pans down. The end of electric operations is exactly a year away. Once electricity ceased to flow in the overhead wires, all of the Y-1's would be sold to the Pennsylvania Railroad.

MONTY POWELL, LOU SCHMITZ COLLECTION

EUGENE VAN DUSEN

ABOVE • Looking as much like an F unit as a Y-1, Y-1a 5011 is at Skykomish on July 4, 1949. The 5011 was wrecked in a derailment at Tonga on March 7, 1945. It was rebuilt with an FT cab on each end and with a streamlined body, resulting in a unique, and highly pleasing, appearance. None of the other Y-1's received this treatment; thus the 5011 was instantly recognizable. Class P-2 4-8-2 #2517 is coupled to the 5011. During World War II, when traffic exceeded the capability of the electrics, the Great Northern would operate steam, diesel and electric locomotives on the same train. Three Y-1's would be placed on the head end of a 6,000-ton train, a four unit set of FT's would be cut in as mid-train helpers and an R-1 or R-2 2-8-8-2 would serve as a rear end helper, cutting off before reaching Cascade Tunnel. Only on the Great Northern! This unusual array of motive power could climb the 2.2% grade to Cascade Tunnel at 17 mph.

BELOW • With the engineer waiting impatiently, the 5011 and 5016 are in Skykomish on July 16, 1956. The 5011 had MU connections mounted on the nose at one end only whereas the other Y-1's had them mounted on the roof on both ends. The maintenance-of-way cars in the background are now mineral red rather than gray. Note the broom at the switch. Although the 5011 was sold to the Pennsylvania Railroad along with the other Y-1's, it never graced Pennsy rails in revenue service as it was used for parts and scrapped in 1957. The two F-unit noses received a keystone and coats of Tuscan red or Brunswick green. One was installed on a wreck damaged E-7 and the other on a FP-7. Perhaps the 5011's aesthetic styling was too flashy for the conservative Pennsy.

EUGENE VAN DUSEN

The 5011 and 5016 move through the yard at Skykomish on July 16, 1956, passing a truss-rodded former box car now in MOW service.

SANFORD GOODRICK

EUGENE VAN DUSEN

SANFORD GOODRICK

ABOVE • After the delivery of the Y-1's in 1927, 1928 and 1930, the Great Northern's electric roster remained stable until after World War II. Freed from wartime restrictions on acquiring new motive power, and with traffic increasing and trains becoming heavier, the GN went shopping for new electric locomotives. In 1947 General Electric delivered two mammoth 5,000 horsepower locomotives, Class W-1, the 5018 and 5019. With a length of 101', a weight of 735,000 pounds, a starting tractive effort of 180,000 pounds, a continuous rating of 5,000 horsepower, and a continuous regenerative breaking capacity of 5,750 horsepower, the W-1's could only be described in superlatives. The most powerful single-unit electrics in the world when built, every axle was powered. With two frames connected at the center, the W-1's had a B-D+D-B wheel arrangement. Heavier, than a Union Pacific "Big Boy", the W-1's could pull a third more than the UP's finest. Geared for 65 mph in freight service, the W's could pull a 2,000-ton train up the 2.2% grade to Cascade Tunnel without helpers and could run downgrade without applying air brakes. The 5018 and 5019 could be run together but could not be MU'd with the other electrics. The 5018 and 5019 rest at Skykomish with pans down on June 10, 1952, five years after their delivery. The influence of diesels clearly shows in the streamlined styling and F-unit style noses.

LEFT • June 16, 1956 appears to be wash day in Skykomish. Sitting at the engine terminal are Y-1a 5011, Y-1 5016 and both W-1's, the 5018 and 5019. In the background are a set of F-units. Once an everyday scene at Skykomish, soon diesels would be the order of the day.

W. C. JANSSEN

ABOVE & BELOW • W-1 #5019 basks in the sunlight at Skykomish on September 5, 1950 with one pantograph raised. The impressive height of the W-1's is evident in the head on view above, while its 101' length is emphasized in a July 16, 1956 view below, at Skykomish.

EUGENE VAN DUSEN

SANFORD GOODRICK

ABOVE • In a classic ¾ view, the 5019 waits for the call to action at Skykomish on July 16, 1956. Behind it is the 5018, several Y-1's and a set of F-units, all adorned in orange and green.

BELOW • W-1 #5019 and an A-B-B-A set of F-3's, led by the 472-D, bring a westbound freight into the Skykomish yard on July 16, 1956 (yes, that is a Great Northern bus to the left of the 5019). The 5019 has a few dents and scrapes on its nose. When the W-1's were delivered in 1947 the Great Northern was still largely a steam railroad. But the GN was rapidly dieselizing its freight operations, first with multi-unit lashups of FT's and later with F-3's and F-7's. The diesels could operate long distances without change, generating dividends in reduced operating costs and considerable time savings. Cutting in and taking out electric locomotives for a 71 mile run was costly in time, labor, and capital investment when diesels could operate long distances. The only barrier to operating diesels across (or through!) the Cascade Range was ventilation of the Cascade Tunnel. When confronted with modernizing and possibly extending electric operations versus adding a new ventilation system to the Cascade Tunnel to allow for dieselization, the economy and standardization offered by diesel-electrics was too great to pass up. Accordingly, the decision was made to terminate electric operations as soon as a new ventilation system was installed. The wires went dead on July 31, 1956, bringing an end to one of the more interesting chapters of "Conquering the Cascades."

EUGENE VAN DUSEN

DISPOSAL OF THE ELECTRICS

JAMES P. SHUMAN

GN 5004A&B
ABOVE • Z-1's 5004A and B sit in a yard devoid of catenary at an unknown location on September 16, 1957. With the end of electrification the Z-1's become orphans. With no home, and nowhere to go, all of the Z's were scrapped, having given the Great Northern the better part of three decades of reliable service.

BELOW • The two W-1's, 5018 and 5019, technologically advanced as they were, found no buyers after the Great Northern terminated electric operations. In 1960 the Union Pacific purchased the 5018 and converted it into a B-unit housing a turbine, part of an experimental coal-fired turbine locomotive. Photographed near Cheyenne, Wyoming on an unknown date, UP 80B operated in the company of UP 80, a converted Alco PA and a tender. Judging by the lack of exhaust, the 80 and 80B have been set up to pose for the company photographer. In April 1964, the former 5018 was renumbered 8080B to make room for newly acquired DD 35's. The coal-fired turbine experiment was declared unsuccessful and the 8080B was scrapped in 1968. The other W-1, 5019, remained on GN rails languishing in the deadline until it was scrapped in Seattle in 1959, an inglorious end to a marvelous locomotive.

UNION PACIFIC RAILROAD

ABOVE • The Pennsylvania Railroad called itself the "Standard Railroad of the World." However, in terms of diesel and electric motive power the Pennsy was anything but. The P Company rarely, if ever, purchased second-hand steam, diesel or electric locomotives (for example, only three purchases of second-hand diesels are on record). However, in 1957 seeking to complete dieselization, the Pennsy was short of motive power and the purchase of the Great Northern Y-1's was seen as an interim solution to the need for new power. When inspecting the Y-1's prior to purchase, the Pennsy folks were amazed at the excellent condition of the venerable workhorses (anyone who spent any time at the Appleyard shops would not have been surprised!). When the purchase was finalized, the Y-1's were shipped east to the Pennsy and shopped at the sprawling Altoona Works for painting and conversion to Pennsylvania Railroad standards. Cab signal equipment was added, the side doors were removed due to tight clearances and the bus jumpers were removed from the roof ends (the Pennsy never had electric locomotives or MU cars connected by 11,000 volts). Y-1 #5014 has just been delivered to the Pennsy's Altoona Works in Altoona, Pennsylvania in 1957. Its bright paint contrasting sharply with the somber hues of the conservative Pennsy, the 5014 will emerge from the shops as PRR #4. The Y-1's had a short life on the Pennsy and #4 was cut up for scrap on June 27, 1960. Parts salvaged from #4 were used to keep #2 running.

BELOW • PRR #6 rests at Thorndale, Pa. on May 2, 1959. Classified as FF-2 by the Pennsy, the Y-1's were orphans from the day they arrived on the Pennsy. The only electrics on the Pennsy to use AC line voltage to drive a motor which rotated a DC generator, the Y-1's high starting tractive effort and very low gear ratio further isolated them. Pennsy engineers, accustomed to the fleet GG-1, had trouble adapting to the FF-2's. Used in helper service, the maximum speed of 35 mph caused problems as the GG-1's or P-5's would often crest the grade in excess of 35 mph, the result being the FF-2 could not gain enough speed to bunch the slack so that the pin could be pulled in order to uncouple. The former Y-1's were all retired by early 1961 and put into storage at the Enola (Pa.) roundhouse. Their final disposition was as follows:

    GN 5010 ....PRR 1, scrapped in 1966
    GN 5011 ....Used for parts
    GN 5012 ....PRR 2, scrapped in March, 1962
    GN 5013 ....PRR 3, scrapped in 1966
    GN 5014 ....PRR 4, scrapped in June, 1960
    GN 5015 ....PRR 5, scrapped in 1966
    GN 5016 ....PRR 6, scrapped in 1966
    GN 5017 ....PRR 7, scrapped in 1966

DON BALL COLLECTION

TOWER CAR

SANFORD GOODRICK

ABOVE • Tower Car X838 was used by the Great Northern to maintain the catenary from Wenatchee to Skykomish. Winter weather and, especially, freezing rain could cause serious problems ranging from coating the wire with ice so the pantographs could not make a connection, to adding weight to the wires so that they were considerably lowered, or worse, broken. The pantographs themselves were not easy on catenary. Aside from normal wear and tear, sometimes a pantograph would become fouled in the catenary with disastrous results. Thus, the catenary needed constant maintenance which ranged from routine preventative maintenance to emergency repairs.

RIGHT • The X838 was built in 1929 by St. Louis Car Company / Mack as a 405 horsepower gas-electric car for passenger postal and express service on lightly used branch lines. Numbered 2337, it had a short life: in 1930 the GN's Jackson Street shops in the Twin Cities converted it to Tower Car X2804. On December 21, 1945 it was renumbered to X838 and in January, 1946, a Cummins diesel engine was installed. Here the X838 is parked on a siding at Leavenworth, Washington on August 22, 1954. Equipped with a headlight on the rear so it could operate without turning, the X838 is seen from the rear on June 12, 1956. Powered by a diesel engine, the X838 was also equipped with a pantograph to ground it when working on line that had not been deenergized.

W. C. JANSSEN

EUGENE VAN DUSEN

ABOVE & BELOW • The X838 had a small glass cupola installed a little more than halfway back on the left side. This allowed for close observation of the catenary in a safe manner, protected from the elements. Seen from the front, the X838 is parked on a siding at Leavenworth on July 16, 1956. The rear end view was taken on August 22, 1954, also at Leavenworth.

SANFORD GOODRICK

127

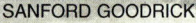

SANFORD GOODRICK

ABOVE • W-1 5019 emerges from the west portal of Cascade Tunnel on July 16, 1956. The train's diesel locomotives remained on the train and once the 5019 cuts off at Skykomish, they will power the train to Seattle. The added labor expense and time required to add or remove electric locomotives was the primary reason for terminating electric locomotives. Had electrification covered a larger area, say west to Seattle, then electric operations would probably have continued for quite some time. Indeed, the Burlington Northern, the Great Northern's corporate successor, conducted feasibility studies on electrifying segments of its lines.

The W-1's were as impressive as the snow-capped Cascades in the background. Indeed, the mountains were the reason the Great Northern needed the W-1's. With their size, enormous tractive effort, and large regenerative braking capacity, the W-1's seemed to be the ideal solution to the Great Northern's efforts to "Conquer the Cascades." The magnificent 5019, posed with the mountains it conquered, illustrates just how great the Great Northern had become. The 5,000 horsepower colossus was a far cry from the diminutive steam locomotives that chugged across the Minnesota prairie during the Great Northern's formative years. Yet even the magnificent W-1's, restricted to operating between Wenatchee and Skykomish, fell victim to changing technology and the Great Northern's never ending quest for greater economy and efficiency. Retired after only nine years of service, the unique W-1's quickly became orphans, leaving us to contemplate the "what ifs" of continued electric operations. The Great Northern would never again roster a locomotive as powerful as the W-1. With the overhead wire devoid of current, multiple unit lashups of diesels took over the electrified district, passing through Skykomish as if it had never existed, ending a fascinating chapter in the Great Northern's history.